*The*
# CIVIL WAR
# DIARY
*of*
# FREEMAN
# COLBY

### FREEMAN'S DEDICATION:

*To Margaret Clement, the one woman, who, as the years passed, became only dearer to me as a friend, sweetheart and wife. No more loyal and helpful, yet sympathetic and lovable woman ever lived than she. She has gone on before me but her memory is ever with me now as it was in all the long war years and it stands now as it did then for all that is truest and best in the world.*

### MAREK'S DEDICATION:

*To Freeman's generation, and all their countless stories yet untold and undrawn.*

*And to my students, who kept asking me, "So, is it done yet?"*

# The *CIVIL WAR DIARY* of
# FREEMAN COLBY

*drawn by* **MAREK BENNETT**
*Live Free And Draw* | **COMICS WORKSHOP** | **2016**

**The Civil War Diary of Freeman Colby**
Drawn by Marek Bennett | www.MarekBennett.com
Published 2016 by **COMICS WORKSHOP** / IngramSpark edition 2019
PAPERBACK ISBN: 978-0-9824153-5-1
HARDCOVER ISBN: 978-0-9824153-6-8

BISAC Subject Codes:
YAN012010 YOUNG ADULT NONFICTION / Comics & Graphic Novels / Biography
YAN012020 YOUNG ADULT NONFICTION / Comics & Graphic Novels / History
YAN025210 YOUNG ADULT NONFICTION / History / U.S. / Civil War Period (1850-1877)

The characters & events depicted here should all be considered creations of the artist, based on primary source texts & images depicting actual historical people & events. For historically accurate quotes & details, please refer to the sources cited in the appendices.

# TABLE OF CONTENTS.

~ Foreword. Maps. ~

**~ APPENDICES: Gallery of Scenes. About the Diary.
Freeman Colby's War Record. Reference Images & Sources. ~**

# FOREWORD.

I first stumbled across Freeman Colby one chilly fall afternoon in 2012. Or rather, Colby stumbled across me, when a typewritten transcript of his diary tumbled into my hands from a dusty archive box at the Henniker Historical Society. I asked local history buffs and teachers about the document; everybody shrugged, nobody had read it. For all I knew, Colby's tale had been sitting unread in that box for the past hundred years, just waiting for new readers to find it...

From his first page, Colby comes across as a true Yankee character with a gripping story to tell. Drawing out that story in comics is my way of trying to understand it. By now, I feel like I've spent a good part of the past few years in Maryland, 1862, right alongside Colby and "Company K" through all those long days and cold nights. I hope this book gives you a similar sense of their world.

The *text* of this book is Freeman Colby's – words, spelling, even punctuation; whenever I made any small changes to suit the comics format, I drew a little squiggle-mark (~) under the panel. The *drawings* are mine, of course with the aid of many reference images (see the Appendix). And the *story*... Well, now it's yours. Ours. Enjoy.

~ Marek / Henniker, NH / 2016

**MAP: COLBY'S NEW ENGLAND**
*Detail from "Map of rail road routes from Rouse's Point to Portsmouth and Boston; compiled for the Cocheco Railroad Co. November, 1848." by George B. Parrott & Cocheco Railroad [LOC.gov].*
❶ Henniker ❷ Woburn ❸ Boxford ❹ Boston

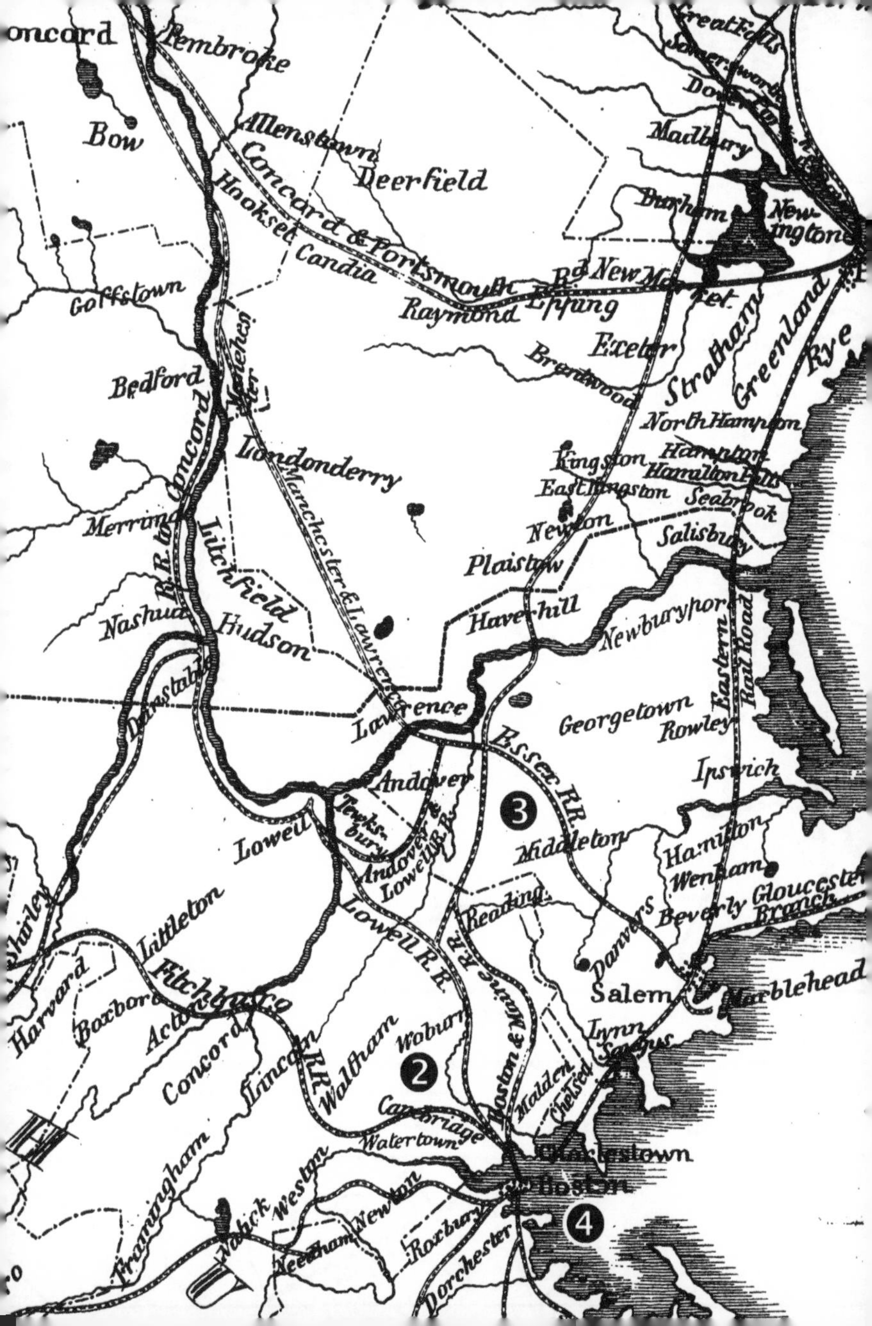

Concord
Pembroke
Bow
Allenstown
Deerfield
Concord & Portsmouth Rd.
Hookset
Candia
Raymond
Epping
New Market
Goffstown
Manchester
Bedford
Concord
Londonderry
Merrimack
R.R. to
Litchfield
Nashua
Hudson
Manchester & Lawrence
Dunstable
Lawrence
Great Falls
Somersworth
Dover
Madbury
Durham
Newington
Exeter
Brentwood
Stratham
Greenland
Rye
North Hampton
Hampton
Hampton Falls
Kingston
East Kingston
Seabrook
Newton
Salisbury
Plaistow
Haverhill
Newburyport
Eastern Rail Road
Georgetown
Rowley
Ipswich
Essex R.R.
Andover
Tewksbury
Andover & Lowell R.R.
Lowell
Middleton
Hamilton
Wenham
Beverly
Gloucester Branch
Reading
Danvers
Lowell R.R.
Boston & Maine R.R.
Salem
Marblehead
Lynn
Saugus
Shirley
Littleton
Harvard
Boxboro
Fitchburg
Acton
Concord
Lincoln
R.R.
Waltham
Woburn
Malden
Chelsea
Cambridge
Watertown
Charlestown
Boston
Framingham
Natick
Weston
Newton
Needham
Roxbury
Dorchester
2
3
4

Berlin

Addamstown

Urbana

U. Point of

Trammelstown Rocks

Three Springs

L. Point of

Rocks

MONOCACY

SUGAR LOAF

Hyattstown

Licksville

Clarksburg

Nolands Ferry

Hauling Ferry

Barnesville

Sen
Br

Waterford

Cheeks Ford

Whites Ford

Monocacy Church

Middlebrook

6

Conrads F.

4

Poolville

Gaither

Clarks Gap

5

LEESBURG

Edwards Ferry

Dorr

Creek

Chesapeake

Seneca

Goose

na

Alexandria R.D.

Gre

Dranesville

### SCALE

10 9 8 7 6 5 4 3 2 1 0                    10 MILES

+++++++++ Rail Roads          ——— Common Roads

═══════ Turnpikes              ∼∼∼ Canals

na

Chantilly

Falls Che

Turnpike

MAP: COLBY'S MARYLAND

*Composite detail from* **"Theatre of operations, Maryland Campaign, September 1862"** *by H. W. Mattern & Ezra Ayers Carman* [LOC.gov].

❶ Washington D.C.  ❷ Arlington
❸ Offutts Crossroads  ❹ Poolville
❺ Edwards Ferry  ❻ Conrads Ferry

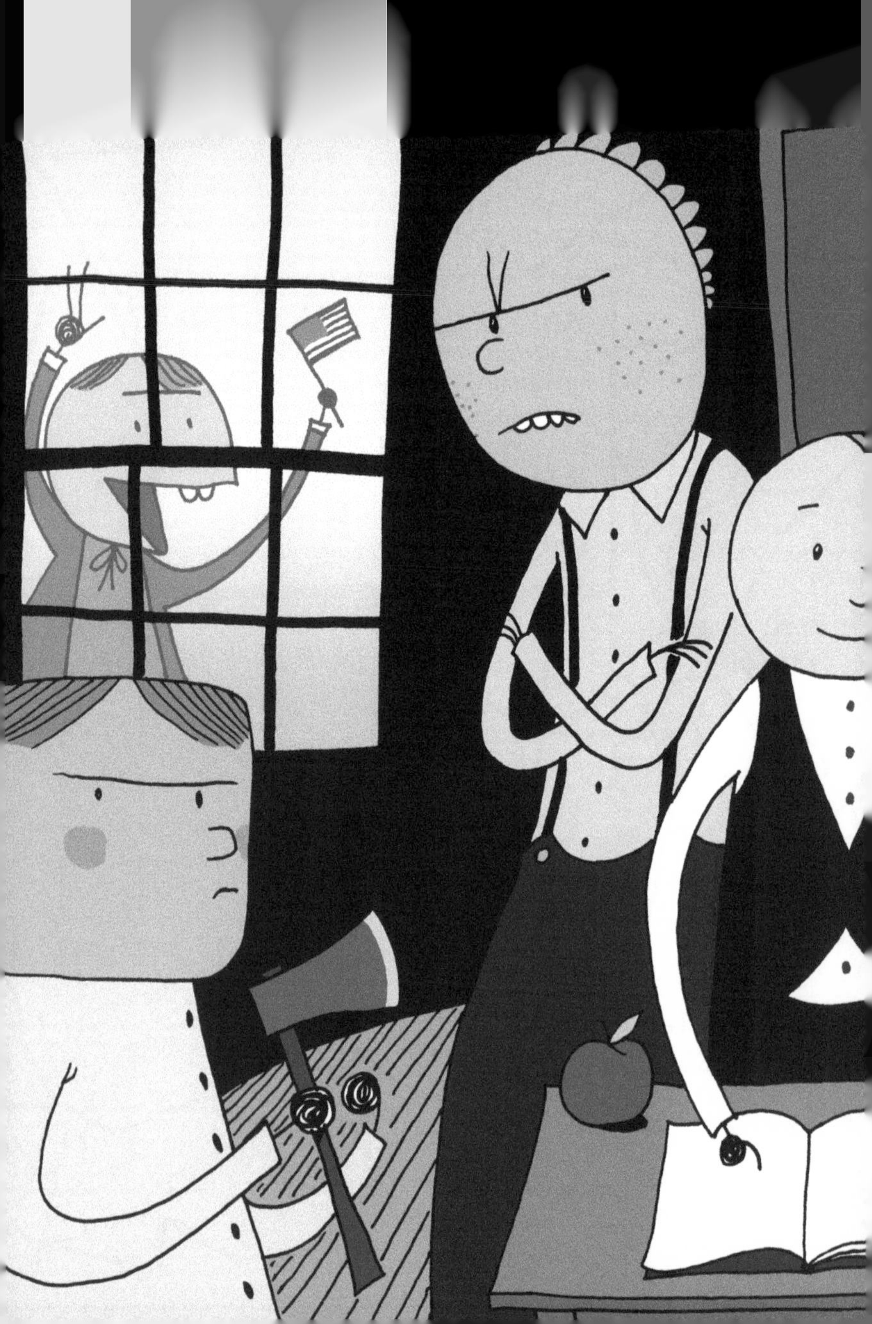

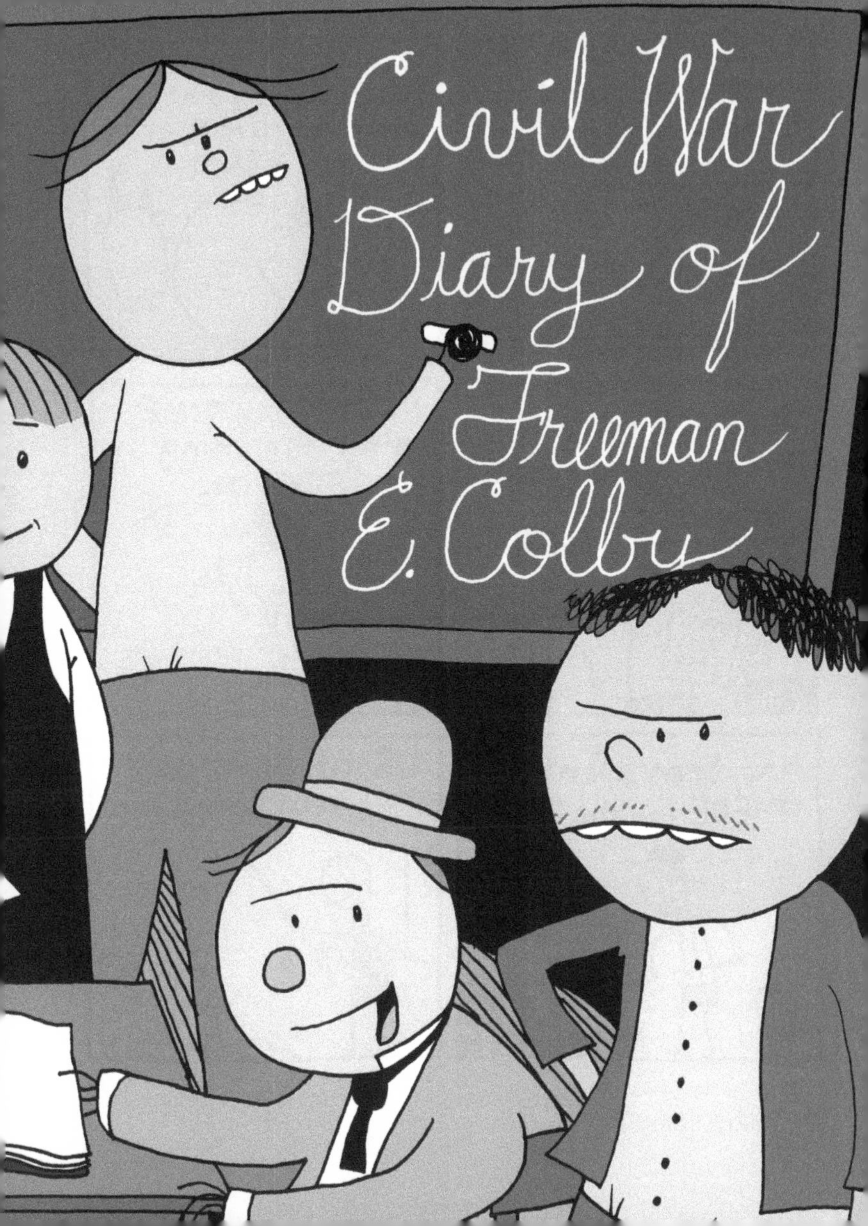
Civil War
Diary of
Freeman
E. Colby

CIVIL WAR DIARY OF FREEMAN E. COLBY

APRIL, 1861
Henniker, NH

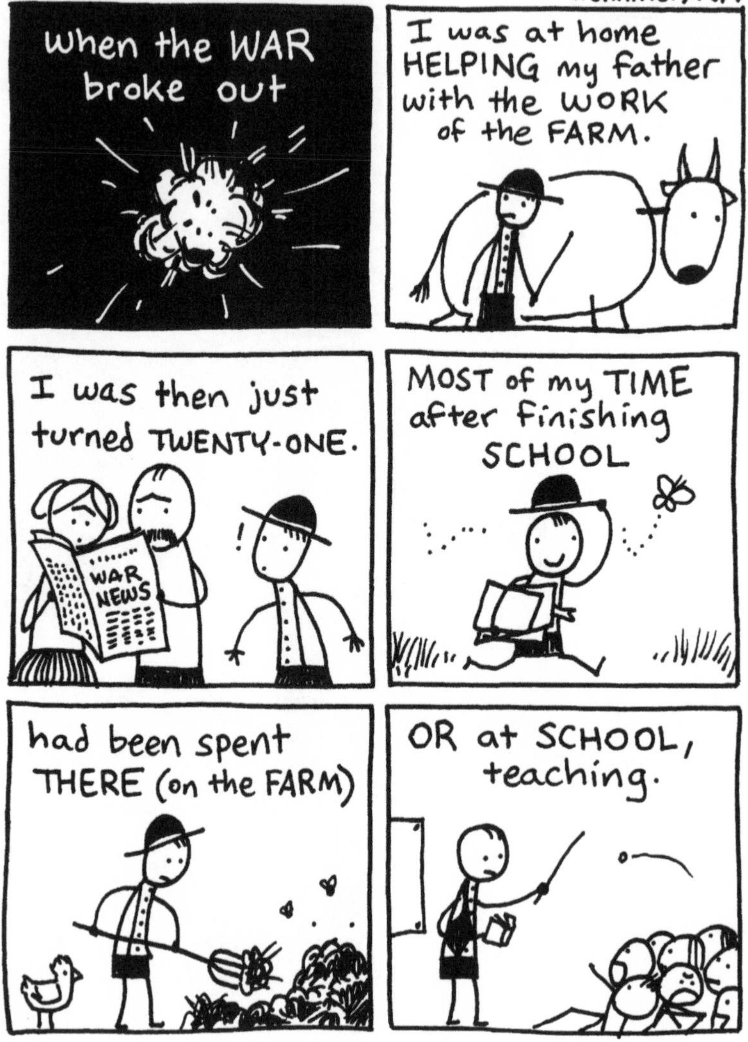
when the WAR broke out
I was at home HELPING my father with the WORK of the FARM.
I was then just turned TWENTY-ONE.
WAR NEWS
!
MOST of my TIME after finishing SCHOOL
had been spent THERE (on the FARM)
OR at SCHOOL, teaching.

AT KEEPING SCHOOL I had had good SUCCESS

and in schools where there were MANY SCHOLARS older and larger than MYSELF,

I had NEVER FAILED to keep ORDER.

SEVERAL TIMES I had FINISHED the terms

OF TEACHERS who had LEFT their schoolrooms by the WINDOWS

and as I tried to be JUST

as well as STRICT,

my SERVICES were IN DEMAND,

PARTICULARLY in districts where each WINTER TERM

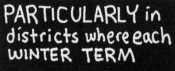

was EXPECTED to Commence with a SET—TO between the MASTER

and a HALF DOZEN or MORE of HUSKY LADS

whose MUSCLES were TOUGHENED

by the use of SCYTHE

FLAIL

and AXE,

and whose ideas of INDEPENDENCE

would not PERMIT them to LEARN

of ONE who could be either FRIGHTENED or LICKED.

There, the <u>MASTER</u>

and not the SCHOLARS

had to STAND being HAZED.

But I was ANXIOUS to get some OPENING that PROMISED BETTER returns...

# HOW RELENTLESS

With the BOMBARDMENT of FORT SUMTER

the whole NORTH AWOKE with a shock

to the EXISTENCE of war;

but FEW of even the BEST INFORMED MEN

dreamed of how RELENTLESS and long DRAWN OUT

that STRUGGLE was to be.

Even the PRESIDENT, in his CALL for VOLUNTEERS,

only specified 30 DAYS as the LENGTH of service.

Men of N.H. ARISE 30 days

# WOBURN

During that SUMMER and FALL

there was PLENTY of work on the FARM for us all

and I only left OCCASIONALLY for TRIPS about the nearby towns

with large and brightly colored PICTURES of FORTS and BATTLE SCENES

which found a READY SALE.

As WINTER came on, MY work was LESS NEEDED at home,

but instead of TAKING a SCHOOL to keep, I went to WOBURN

and got a JOB in a CURRIER SHOP.

A former classmate and neighbor named JONAS BACON

worked there TOO

but besides HIM and some of his RELATIVES (with whom I went to BOARD)

I knew NO ONE in the town.

RETTA

I was never OVER READY

to make NEW FRIENDS

but during that WINTER at WOBURN I met...

MARGARET CLEMENT

who was then learning the TAILOR'S TRADE.

WAR NEWS
NEW ORLEANS SURRENDERS!
ON TO RICHMOND
DECISIVE BATTLE?

# NEWTON

| | | |
|---|---|---|
| With LINCOLN'S first call for troops in 1861,  | NEWTON (my brother) 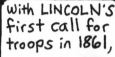 | was at once WILD to JOIN the army.  |
| He was only 17 then  | and everyone told him he was TOO YOUNG to enlist  | but as TIME PASSED he only became MORE EAGER to go.  |
| Early in the SUMMER of 1862, Mother and Father SAW  | that IN SPITE of ALL they could SAY,  | he was BOUND to ENLIST  |
| and would RUN AWAY and JOIN  | some one of the many REGIMENTS being RAISED...  | WITHOUT their CONSENT if they continued to WITHOLD it.  |

# WE ENLISTED

It was also in MY mind to ENLIST

So when they WROTE to me of their TROUBLE,

I readily CONSENTED to their PLAN

that we should ENLIST ToGETHER!

He was TWO YEARS my junior

and had NEVER been AWAY from home... more than a few DAYS at a time.

The 39th REGIMENT of MASSACHUSETTS VOLUNTEERS

was being RAISED just then

with COLONEL P. Stearns DAVIS as COMMANDER.

19 of my SHOPMATES enlisted in COMPANY K

and the balance of the company was made up of WOBURN MEN.

I WROTE HOME about it

and Newton CAME DOWN

and ENLISTED with me.

He PROMISED mother and father

to come to ME for ADVICE and COUNSEL

(WHENEVER I was at hand)

and I, in turn,

was charged to LOOK AFTER his WELFARE

as much as POSSIBLE.

We ENLISTED July 22, 1862 at WOBURN

and Jonas JOINED at the SAME TIME.

# TEETH

We were first EXAMINED by the SURGEON,

who gave us a TEST much like an EXAMINATION for insurance

except that it included a CRITICAL INSPECTION of the TEETH.

We had heard of the terrors of HARDTACK

and now we learned that the SURGEON would NOT PASS a man

who had LOST 2 or 3 TEETH.

This seemed HIGHHANDED and UNREASONABLE,

but we found LATER ON

that ALL the GRINDERS Nature had GIVEN US

were none too MANY or too GOOD,

for the ARMY RATIONS taxed their capacity to the LIMIT

and we no longer WONDERED that a FULL SET was one of the REQUIREMENTS. ....

## MEASURING UP

We were MEASURED and an accurate RECORD was made...
↕ height— ~age color of eyes and hair //// weight— build

All this, together with NAMES and ADDRESS of each man's PARENTS

was FILED AWAY for use in IDENTIFYING him

in case he should DIE

* or DESERT

or be TAKEN PRISONER

I remember that MY HEIGHT was RECORDED as an INCH and a HALF MORE
5'8½?!

than it ever was BEFORE or has been SINCE.
I wonder WHY....?

# COMPANY K

| | | |
|---|---|---|
| After SIGNING the Regimental roll  | We were all 3 ASSIGNED to COMPANY K  | under Captain JOHN I. RICHARDSON.  |
| HERE we were entirely among WOBURN MEN...  | JONAS and I knew but FEW of them  | while to NEWTON they were ALL STRANGERS.  |
| ...but MOST of them had been NEIGHBORS at .... HOME and before long they formed LITTLE GROUPS  | Who ATE, SLEPT, and MARCHED  | as much as possible TOGETHER. |

# CAMP LIFE

Camp life was a ROUTINE of CALLS,

DRILLS,

MEALS,

DRILLS,

DETAILS for the WORK of the camp,

and still more DRILLS.

It was the HOTTEST of DOG-DAY WEATHER, too,

but still we didn't much MIND the ETERNAL PRACTICE

because it was NEW to US...

At first we had to wear our USUAL CLOTHES

but as soon as UNIFORMS, GUNS and the various ARTICLES of EQUIPMENT

could be OBTAINED from the Government...

U.S.

and from the CONTRACTORS,

they were ISSUED to the MEN,

and EACH article,

even to the WOODEN PLUG for the MUZZLE of his GUN

was CHARGED UP with MILITARY PRECISION

to the MAN who RECEIVED it.

# WARES

MANY of the men were but a FEW MILES from their HOMES

So there was MUCH VISITING back and forth

and EVERY DAY the camp was THRONGED

with FRIENDS and RELATIVES of the boys,

SIGHTSEERS,

and VENDERS of PIES, cakes, fruit, CUTLERY,

and many SMALL WARES

which each dealer ASSURED his customers

would be ABSOLUTELY NECESSARY

to their HEALTH and COMFORT at the FRONT.

Many of the boys LOADED UP with these articles...

until they needed a DONKEY apiece to CARRY their LUGGAGE.

# LEAVE

DISCIPLINE was not very STRICT

and MOST of the men could OCCASIONALLY get LEAVE to go HOME.

When we ENLISTED, Captain RICHARDSON

PROMISED each man in K Company: "...one week's FURLOUGH before we leave the state!" YAAAY!

He was a NORTH WOBURN man

and NO SOONER were we IN CAMP

then the boys from HIS town

Commenced to get LEAVE to go HOME

for a FEW DAYS at a time

and some of them SPENT MORE TIME at Woburn

than they did with the REGIMENT.

# CLOSE TO HOME

Several times parties of THREE to SIX

CHIPPED IN together

to hire a pair of HORSES and a DEMOCRAT WAGON

for the DRIVE over HOME (which was only about 16 MILES away)

Woburn

They usually STARTED after the day's WORK was DONE

and RETURNED with the team the next MORNING,

but if any of them HAD LEAVE to stay LONGER than that,

there were always OTHERS ready to take their places on the TRIP BACK.

They usually BROUGHT BACK with them

a STOCK of EATABLES

and a LIBERAL SUPPLY of LIQUID REFRESHMENTS

OTHERS had HAMPERS and BOXES

of GOOD THINGS to EAT and DRINK sent to them—

Sometimes with more GENEROSITY than DISCRETION.

In this way, we had many TREATS

to HOME COOKED FOOD,

which VARIED the FARE of the CAMP

(though this was mainly very GOOD).

# DRILLING

But most of our TIME was devoted to DRILLING

which was MOST NECESSARY

for NONE of us had any MILITARY EXPERIENCE

and OFFICERS and MEN ALIKE must KNOW

the "MANUAL of ARMS" in Casey's TACTICS

and become FAMILIAR with COMPANY and REGIMENTAL evolutions

before they could be of ANY USE

to the COUNTRY they had ENLISTED to DEFEND.

Some took the TRAINING with sober INDUSTRY

and diligently tried to LEARN all they could,

while OTHERS never realized until LONG AFTERWARDS

that it was ANYTHING but a PICNIC FROLIC.

# REFUSAL

No one could tell HOW LONG we would have for PRACTICE

but RUMORS were RIFE that made it fairly SURE we had NO GREAT TIME to wait

before commencing ACTIVE SERVICE.

JONAS and I had been repeatedly REFUSED PERMISSION

to go over to WOBURN or even to LEAVE the CAMP.

NEWTON was having a FINE TIME and had NO WISH to be away from the REGIMENT

but WE wanted to GO HOME while we could

So we ASKED the CAPTAIN for the promised WEEK'S FURLOUGH.

He CURTLY REFUSED us.

We had then been in CAMP about SIX WEEKS

and as the REGIMENT as a whole was getting fairly USED TO

the MANEUVERS of the PARADE GROUND

WE felt that the TIME was getting SHORT.

We TALKED the matter over between OURSELVES

and as we were plainly ENTITLED to the FURLOUGH,

we determined to TAKE IT in SPITE of the Captain's REFUSAL.

The CAMP was near a POND a little east of the BOXFORD RAILROAD STATION

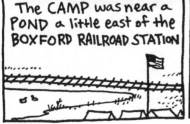

and where the CAMPGROUND bordered the TRACK there was a FINE GRASSY BANK

where the MEN used to LOUNGE when off duty,

especially as TRAIN TIME approached.

We carefully LAID our PLANS

and ONE DAY about the FIRST of SEPTEMBER we placed ourselves among the REST

and just as a TRAIN was pulling out of the STATION TOWARDS BOSTON

WE JUMPED UP

and MADE a DASH for the REAR CAR.

Perhaps the CAPTAIN had SUSPECTED

that something besides CURIOSITY brought us there

for he was NEARBY

and RAN to HEAD us OFF.

we barely GAINED the rear steps

and DREW ourselves UP by them,

but the CAPTAIN, who had FARTHER to run

fell JUST SHORT as the train INCREASED its SPEED

so in another MINUTE he was LEFT BEHIND,

WAVING his arms

and SHOUTING for the TRAIN to be STOPPED.

He TELEGRAPHED to Boston

to have us ARRESTED when we got off the train THERE

but we had this in mind

and GOT OFF at a small town — I think it was WAKEFIELD —

and took a HORSECAR to WINCHESTER

where we GOT ON a Boston & Lowell train for NEW HAMPSHIRE.

We went STRAIGHT to HENNIKER

And spent the MOST of our WEEK THERE,

Enjoying EVERY HOUR of it.

As the TIME was so SHORT, I could not CALL ON more than a FEW

of the many I WANTED to SEE,

but I DID go over to UNCLE HENRY PIPER's at Bradford

and TALKED OVER the WAR and POLITICAL PROSPECTS with him

and with AUNT ABBIE, who was JUST as keenly INTERESTED in all the NEWS...

I PROMISED to WRITE them as OFTEN as I could.

UNCLE ROBERT HARRIMAN was another who took an INTEREST in POLITICS,

BUT as he was a DEMOCRAT, we were very FAR from AGREEING.

...If I had WRITTEN REGULARLY to ALL THOSE who ASKED me to do so,

My SPARE TIME would ALL have been TAKEN UP with PEN and INK.

# FAREWELL

It was a BUSY WEEK and when it was NEARLY UP

I said GOODBYE to MOTHER and FATHER

and the GIRLS

FOLLOWED by their tearful FAREWELLS and good WISHES

and charges to LOOK OUT for NEWTON (all I could)

AND to take good care of MYSELF.

NO ONE could tell WHEN I would SEE THEM again,

if EVER.

JONAS joined me at the STATION

and we went DIRECTLY to WOBURN

where we heard OUR REGIMENT was to BREAK CAMP at Boxford NEXT MORNING

~

and GO at once to WASHINGTON.

But OUR TIME was not UP until the NEXT DAY

So I spent the EVENING with RETTA*

*fiancee Margaret Clement

and next morning JONAS and I went to BOSTON together.

It being then TOO LATE to go to BOXFORD,

We decided to MEET the REGIMENT when it ARRIVED in BOSTON.

We spent a BUSY FORENOON trying to BUY

the FEW THINGS we KNEW we would NEED...

and I LAID IN a small stock of TOOLS for REPAIRING WATCHES.

When the regiment FILED from the CARS

in the HAYMARKET SQUARE railroad station

and FELL INTO LINE for the MARCH across the city,

WE took our PLACES in the RANKS with the rest.

# GETTING BACK

And NOW it was Captain Richardson's TURN to GET BACK at US

for "RUNNING AWAY" (as HE chose to call it).

TO US, it had been a HUGE JOKE to OUTWIT HIM ........

and take our INFORMAL LEAVE of ABSENCE without his PERMISSION

We had had MANY a LAUGH at the MEMORY

of the LUDICROUS FIGURE he cut on the TRACKS at Boxford

after VAINLY CHASING US

to the very CAR STEPS

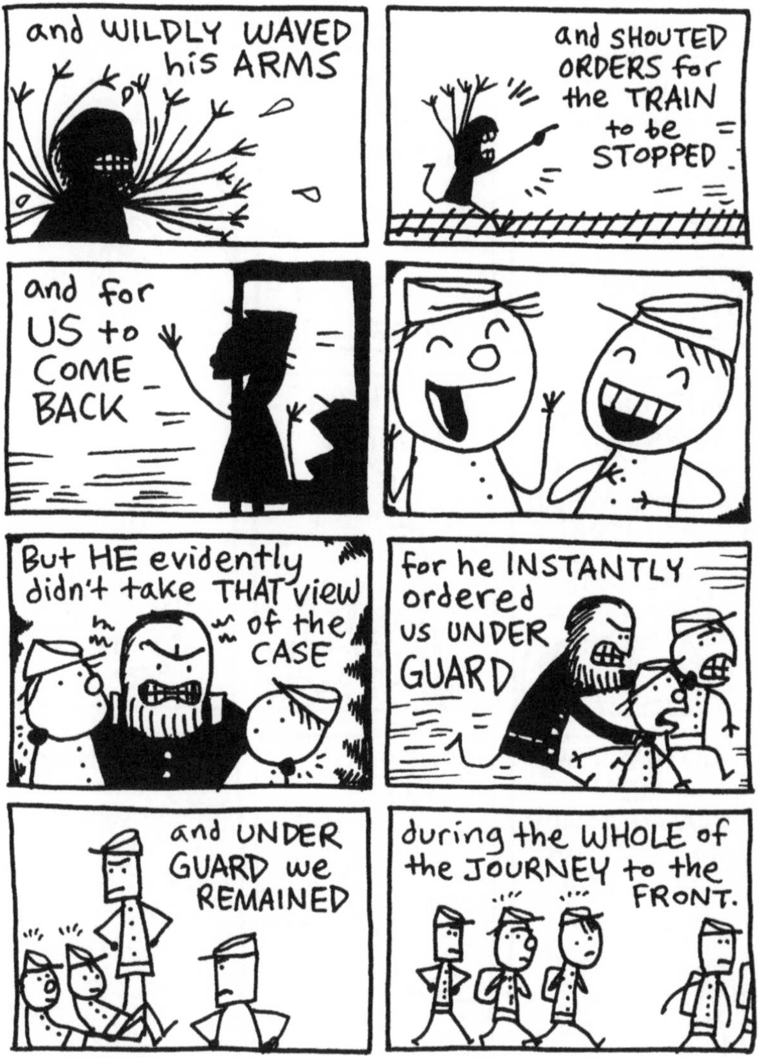
and WILDLY WAVED his ARMS
and SHOUTED ORDERS for the TRAIN to be STOPPED
and for US to COME BACK
But HE evidently didn't take THAT view of the CASE
for he INSTANTLY ordered us UNDER GUARD
and UNDER GUARD we REMAINED
during the WHOLE of the JOURNEY to the FRONT.

## DROPPING OUT

The distance from HAYMARKET SQUARE

to the WORCESTER STATION (on Beech Street)

was only about a MILE

BUT we were PARADED up and down Boston's MAZE of streets

for THREE HOURS

The day was HOT

and MANY of the MEN, UNACCUSTOMED to carrying a FULL LOAD

DROPPED OUT

and made their way ACROSS by the SHORTEST CUT they could FIND.

We left BOSTON at three thirty

and got to NEW LONDON (CT) at NINE in the EVENING.

Our BAGGAGE had not come

So the NEW YORK BOAT waited for it

and the WHOLE REGIMENT had to SPEND the TIME as best they could

Until ELEVEN o'clock

inside the GUARDS that were kept AROUND US

for FEAR, I suppose, that some of us might DESERT.

# PROGRESS

We reached JERSEY CITY at half past seven SUNDAY morning.

There we were put on a TRAIN again

and got to PHILADELPHIA at two in the afternoon.

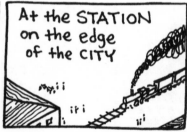

At the STATION on the edge of the CITY

the TRAIN WAS STOPPED

and we were ORDERED to get OUT of the CARS

and FORM in LINE

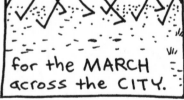

for the MARCH across the CITY.

When we got to the GROUND we FOUND

that the ENGINE had been TAKEN from the train

and a LONG STRING of MULES hitched on in its place.

NO ENGINES were allowed within the CITY LIMITS

So ALL the TRAINS were PULLED across by MULE TEAMS

to the STATION on the other SIDE

At a WORD,

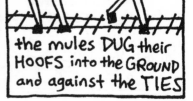

the mules DUG their HOOFS into the GROUND and against the TIES

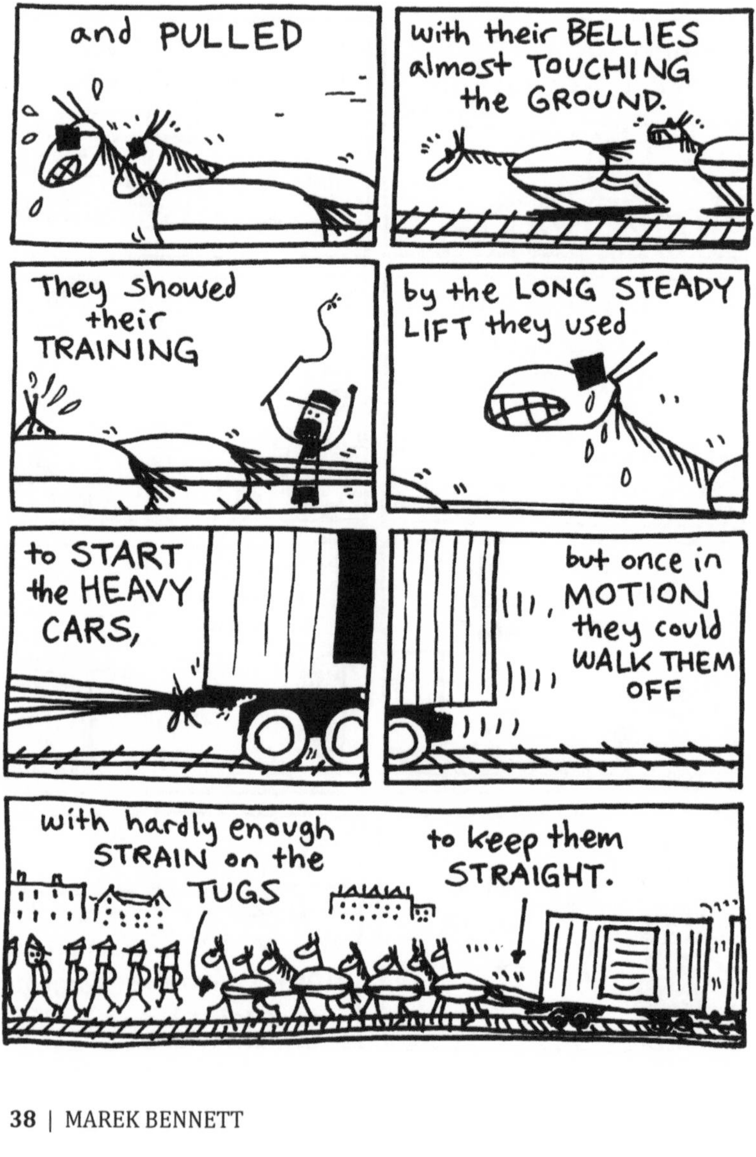
and PULLED
with their BELLIES almost TOUCHING the GROUND.
They showed their TRAINING
by the LONG STEADY LIFT they used
to START the HEAVY CARS,
but once in MOTION they could WALK THEM OFF
with hardly enough STRAIN on the TUGS
to keep them STRAIGHT.

We took DINNER

at the UNION VOLUNTEER REFRESHMENT SALOON

where ALL Union soldiers were FED

at the EXPENSE of the LOYAL CITIZENS

We had had but ONE MEAL since leaving BOSTON

So THIS ONE was VERY acceptable.

TWO of these EATING SALOONS were kept OPEN

NIGHT and DAY all through the WAR...

Every FIRE ENGINE COMPANY in the city also had an AMBULANCE

and at the CALL of the BELL which was RUNG WHENEVER a troop train ARRIVED,

these were DRIVEN to MEET it

and the SICK were CARRIED to a HOSPITAL

to be CARED FOR.

Over TWENTY THOUSAND SOLDIERS were cared for there in all.

The SAME BELL also called the WOMEN VOLUNTEERS

who TURNED OUT NIGHT or DAY, whenever it was RUNG

to GATHER at the SALOONS

and MAKE READY the FOOD and COFFEE

for the HUNGRY TROOPS.

# BALTIMORE

At seven in the MORNING we arrived at BALTIMORE.

THIS city IMPRESSED me as a DIRTY SMOKY place

with STREETS almost as IRREGULAR as those of BOSTON ...

At THIS TIME —and indeed ALL THROUGH the WAR—

BALTIMORE was a HOTBED of REBELLION

and we SOON got a TASTE of its QUALITY.

HERE, as in other places we had BEEN THROUGH

People came out of their HOUSES with COFFEE and FOOD

to OFFER US as we MARCHED ALONG

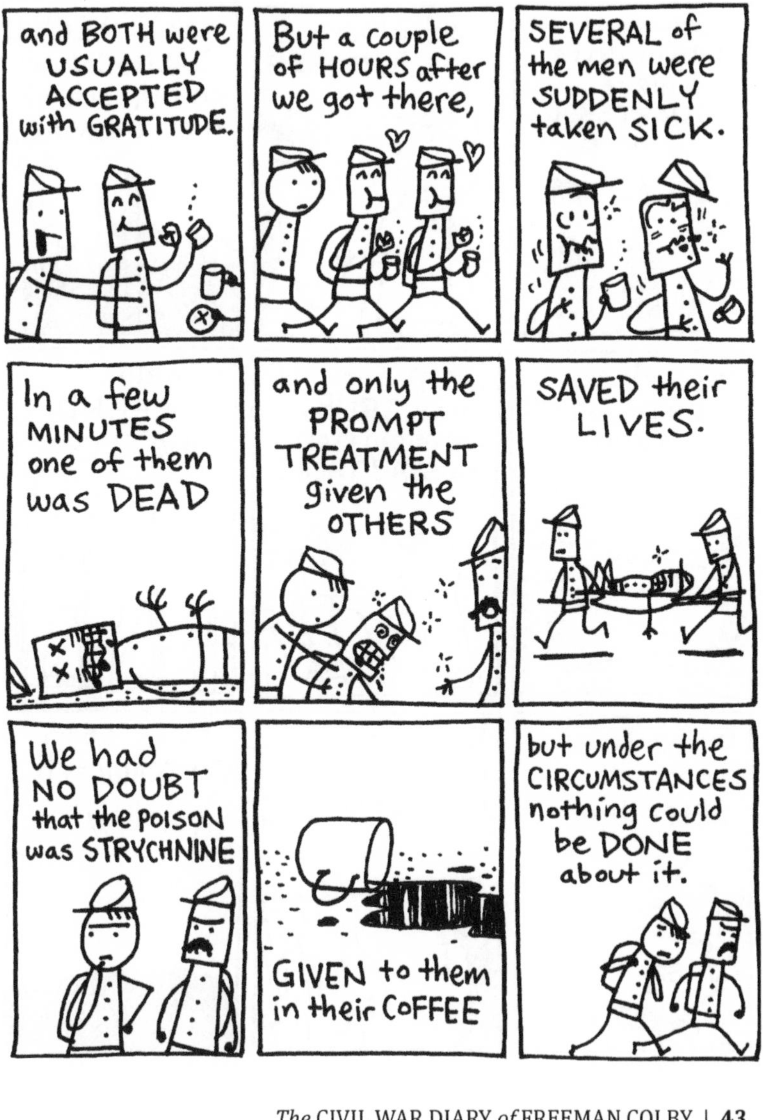
and BOTH were USUALLY ACCEPTED with GRATITUDE.
But a couple of HOURS after we got there,
SEVERAL of the men were SUDDENLY taken SICK.
In a few MINUTES one of them was DEAD
and only the PROMPT TREATMENT given the OTHERS
SAVED their LIVES.
We had NO DOUBT that the POISON was STRYCHNINE
GIVEN to them in their COFFEE
but under the CIRCUMSTANCES nothing could be DONE about it.

# RUMORS

Several regiments were QUARTERED here

and when it was RUMORED

that STONEWALL JACKSON was on OUR side of the POTOMAC,

less than THIRTY MILES away

AND, if it was TRUE, we might expect to STAY THERE

to help DEFEND the CITY

or perhaps GO OUT after him.

But like MOST of the TALES we kept hearing,

it was soon CONTRADICTED.

While we were WAITING for the NEXT MOVE

I BOUGHT a sheet of PAPER

and picking UP a BRICK to WRITE on,

PENCILED a brief ACCOUNT of our journey SO FAR to the HOME FOLKS

ENDING with the comforting ASSURANCE that IF we were POISONED

We would surely ESCAPE being SHOT.

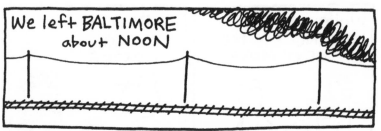

We left BALTIMORE about NOON

and got to WASHINGTON at HALF PAST THREE

There we were at once MARCHED to the BARRACKS

where we were QUARTERED over night

and FED on stale SOFT BREAD

and DAMAGED PORK.

# WASHINGTON

Early next morning we MARCHED SIX MILES through PENNSYLVANIA AVENUE and THIRTEENTH STREET,

across the BRIDGE a MILE in length,

and up to ARLINGTON HEIGHTs where we camped.

AFTER DINNER, Jonas and I, with most of the regiment,

were PUT TO WORK on a FORT.

NEWTON was sent to a FIELD HOSPITAL soon after we arrived at the HEIGHTS.

He had not stood the JOURNEY at all WELL

but he was not ALONE in that

for FOUR OTHERS from the regiment were sent there at the SAME TIME.

As we WORKED on the FORT the whole city of WASHINGTON lay SPREAD OUT before us in the distance beyond the POTOMAC.

About a mile away, at the SUMMIT of the Heights,

stood FORT ELLSWORTH,

named for COLONEL ELLSWORTH of the NEW YORK FIRE ZOUAVES,

who was SHOT

in an ALEXANDRIA hotel,

the FIRST Union soldier KILLED in the WAR.

| | | |
|---|---|---|
| NEARBY was the HOMESTEAD of ROBERT E. LEE 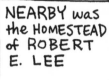 | and FORT ELLSWORTH stood on the SPOT  | where HE had ADVISED the CONSTRUCTION 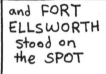 |
| of a CONFEDERATE BATTERY  | for BOMBARDING the city of WASHINGTON.  | THIS was the first REDOUBT built by OUR troops.  |
| NEAR it  | were four OTHER FORTS,  | all COMMANDING the APPROACHES to the CITY.  |

It was thought that THESE FORTS

with the many other BATTERIES in different places

and the HUNDREDS OF THOUSANDS of TROOPS

quartered IN and ABOUT Washington,

made it SECURE from the ATTACK

of ANY CONFEDERATE FORCE then in the field.

But the REBEL LINES were not far away

and the day before WE ARRIVED,

the SECOND BATTLE of BULL RUN* was fought

only TWENTY MILES away.

* Second Manassas (AUG. 29-30, 1862)

Early that morning THREE REGIMENTS had MARCHED from the Heights

to BURY the DEAD.

These they SAID on their RETURN

NUMBERED about FIFTEEN HUNDRED.

There had also been a SKIRMISH

and a DOZEN men KILLED

at CHAIN BRIDGE

six miles UP the RIVER.

# IN CAMP

We ARRIVED at ARLINGTON HEIGHTS the morning of TUESDAY, September 9.

One EVENING two or three days afterward,

there was a VISITOR in CAMP who seemed WELL ACQUAINTED with the WOBURN men

and I heard one of them call him

RODNEY.

Now, I KNEW that my FIANCEE RETT's older sister, JANE, married RODNEY FLAGG,

and that HE had ENLISTED in the 22nd MASS.

54 | MAREK BENNETT

So when I had the CHANCE, I INTRODUCED myself: Is your name not FLAGG?

He seemed PLEASED to MEET ME

and we had a FEW MINUTES pleasant TALK

before he went BACK to his REGIMENT. Yawn!

As he had NOT been PAID OFF and was IN NEED of them,

I GAVE him some WRITING PAPER and a pair of STOCKINGS.

# FALL IN LINE

On SUNDAY, September 14, about FIVE P.M.,

while Jonas and I were WASHING our SHIRTS and OURSELVES

in a little CREEK

we were CALLED to the CAMP

and WITHOUT RATIONS, were given TWO CAMP KETTLES, one full of COFFEE and one full of SUGAR,

on a POLE

and ORDERED to FALL IN LINE for a NIGHT'S MARCH.

EVERYONE was TIRED of working on the FORT

and GLAD to LEAVE it behind.

We ALL felt sure

that our ACTIVE SERVICE was just about to COMMENCE

and NEARLY ALL were in the BEST of SPIRITS at the prospect.

# MARCHING

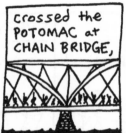

We marched up toward ALEXANDRIA,

crossed the POTOMAC at CHAIN BRIDGE,

and then FOLLOWED the HIGHWAY

on the MARYLAND side of the RIVER

leaving WASHINGTON behind us.

The WEATHER was HOT and SULTRY

and the roads ANKLE DEEP with DUST

which HUNG about us in a CLOUD as we went along

so ALL but the men in FRONT

had to BREATHE it as well as WALK in it.

Koff
koff koff koff

Though the AIR COOLED OFF a little after DARK,

the MEN were TIRED by that time, so the RELIEF was SMALL.

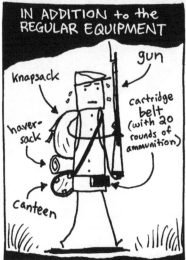

IN ADDITION to the REGULAR EQUIPMENT

gun

knapsack

haver-sack

cartridge belt (with 20 rounds of ammunition)

Canteen

all together WEIGHING close to SIXTY POUNDS

MANY of them were BURDENED with BUNDLES they had brought from HOME.

THESE and all the rest who were NOT in the BEST of CONDITION

soon began to LAG.

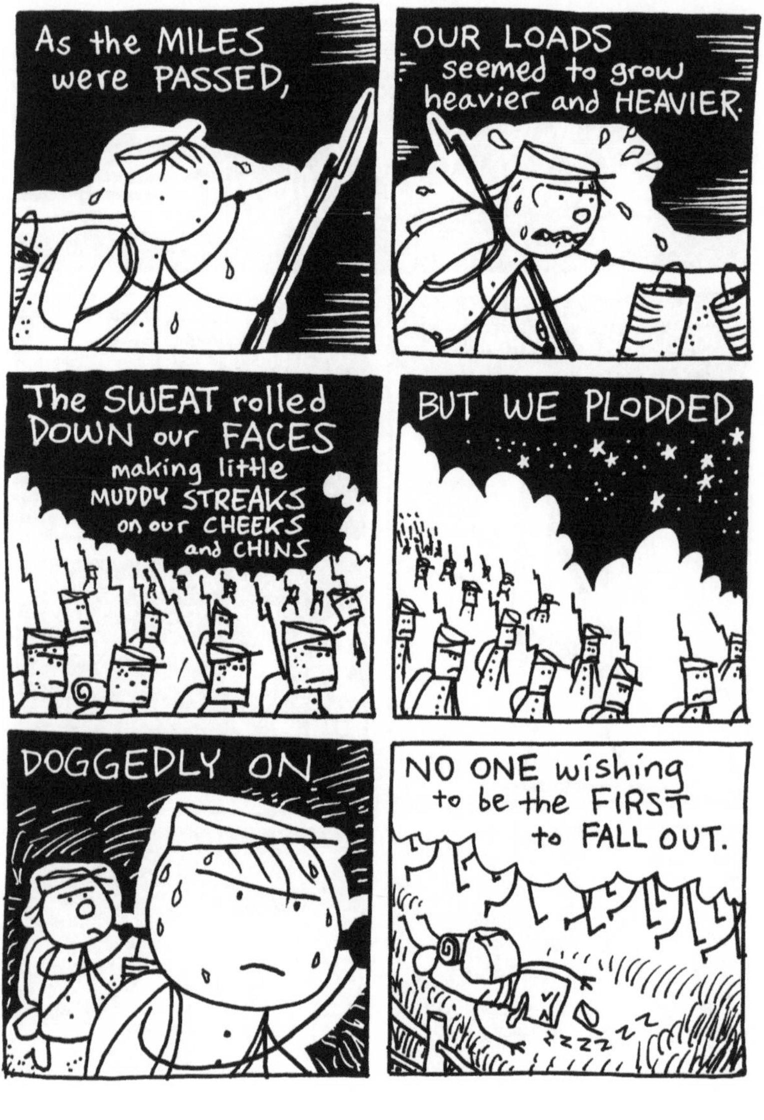
As the MILES were PASSED,
OUR LOADS seemed to grow heavier and HEAVIER.
The SWEAT rolled DOWN our FACES making little MUDDY STREAKS on our CHEEKS and CHINS
BUT WE PLODDED
DOGGEDLY ON
NO ONE wishing to be the FIRST to FALL OUT.
ZZZZ Z Z

EACH ONE thought over the different THINGS he was CARRYING

and to be RID OF the WEIGHT, CONCLUDED to TRY and GET ALONG WITHOUT some of them.

ARTICLES given them by FRIENDS at home

or that had been BOUGHT to add to their COMFORTS in CAMP

and had been VALUED HIGHLY a few HOURS before

were now OFFERED as GIFTS to their COMRADES.

*The* CIVIL WAR DIARY *of* FREEMAN COLBY | **61**

But there were BUT FEW takers

and ONE BY ONE bundles of EXTRA PROVISIONS, brought along to HELP OUT the rations,

were THROWN aside,

THEN followed EXTRA CLOTHES

and a THOUSAND SMALL ARTICLES

until AT LAST little was left but the REGULAR equipment.

SOME even THREW AWAY the CARTRIDGES out of their belts.

EVEN THEN our loads

seemed MANY TIMES HEAVIER than when we started.

STRAGGLING COMMENCED early in the evening

for though PRIDE may KEEP a man IN LINE

WHILE his strength LASTS,

there WILL come a TIME

when his TIRED LEGS

will REFUSE to BEAR him any farther.

Before ELEVEN O'CLOCK, only 18 MEN out of our company* REMAINED in LINE.

*COMPANY = ~100 men

THE REST were STRETCHED OUT beside the road

ZZZZZZZ

or PLODDING ALONG behind.

X!¿#!  X!¿#!  X#!

About this time JONAS and I were RELIEVED of our EXTRA LOADS

and SOON AFTER we SLIPPED our guards,

CRAWLED through a FENCE,

unrolled our BLANKETS

and went to SLEEP.

EARLY NEXT MORNING we started along again

and found the REGIMENT in CAMP about a MILE further on.

CAPTAIN RICHARDSON was very ANGRY

and made some THREATS to us

then SENT US, again under GUARD,

to UNLOAD a canal boat,

where we WORKED until ONE P.M.

Here we got a BOILED DINNER of the toll man

for which we each PAID FIFTY CENTS,

but when it was HALF EATEN we were SUMMONED to CAMP

Our GUARDS ORDERED us to FALL IN but we PAID NO HEED to them

until the DINNER was FINISHED

when we went back to the CAMP as QUICK as we could.

The REGIMENT was IN LINE when we got there

and the CAPTAIN gave us a SWEET BLESSING,

besides our EXTRA LOAD,

and we AGAIN started on the MARCH.

STILL FOLLOWING up the POTOMAC with the BALTIMORE AND OHIO CANAL near us on our left.

We arrived at POOLVILLE sometime after DARK

in a SEVERE RAIN STORM

having MARCHED over THIRTY MILES since leaving ARLINGTON HEIGHTS Sunday afternoon.

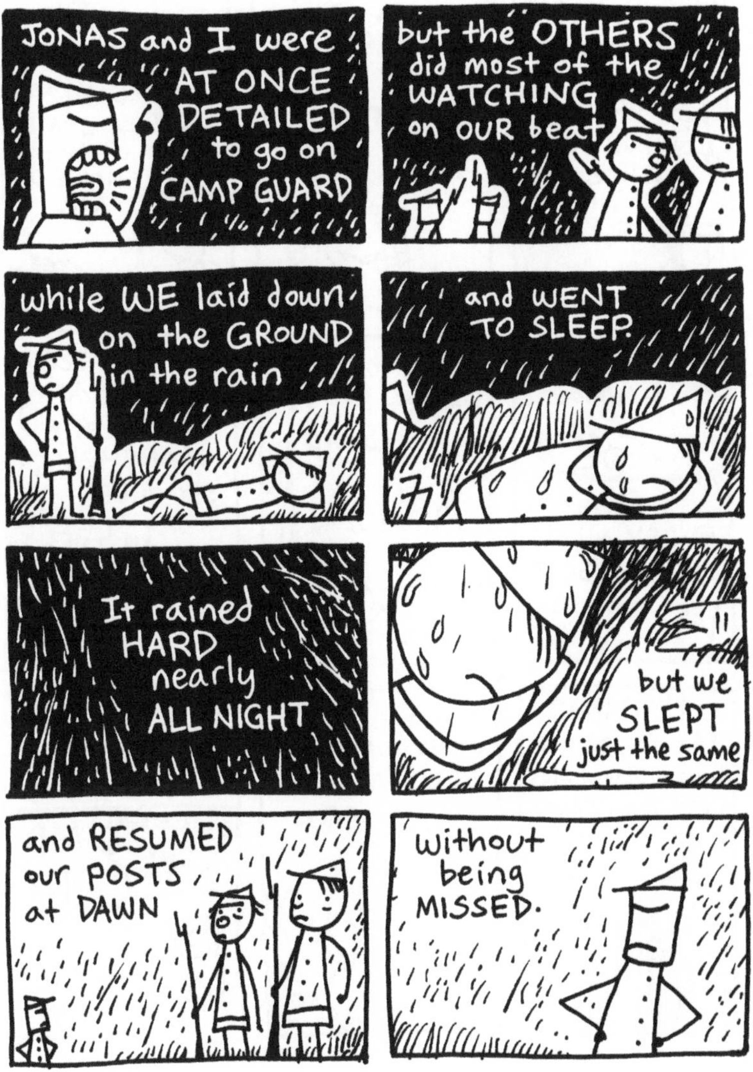
JONAS and I were AT ONCE DETAILED to go on CAMP GUARD
but the OTHERS did most of the WATCHING on OUR beat
while WE laid down on the GROUND in the rain
and WENT TO SLEEP.
It rained HARD nearly ALL NIGHT
but we SLEPT just the same
and RESUMED our POSTS at DAWN
without being MISSED.

With **DAYLIGHT** the **STRAGGLERS** who had **DROPPED OUT** of line the **NIGHT BEFORE**

commenced to **COME INTO CAMP** by **TWOS** and **THREES**.

The **DAY** was **WELL ALONG** before **SOME** of them **SHOWED UP**.

**MANY** were **LAME** and almost **EVERY MAN** was **FOOTSORE**.

After our **DAY** of **REST** in camp

We started Wednesday morning and **MARCHED SIX MILES**

to **EDWARDS FERRY**, where five companies went into **CAMP**

and the rest of us went **STILL FARTHER** on,

to **TAKE** our **PLACES** in the **PICKET LINE**.

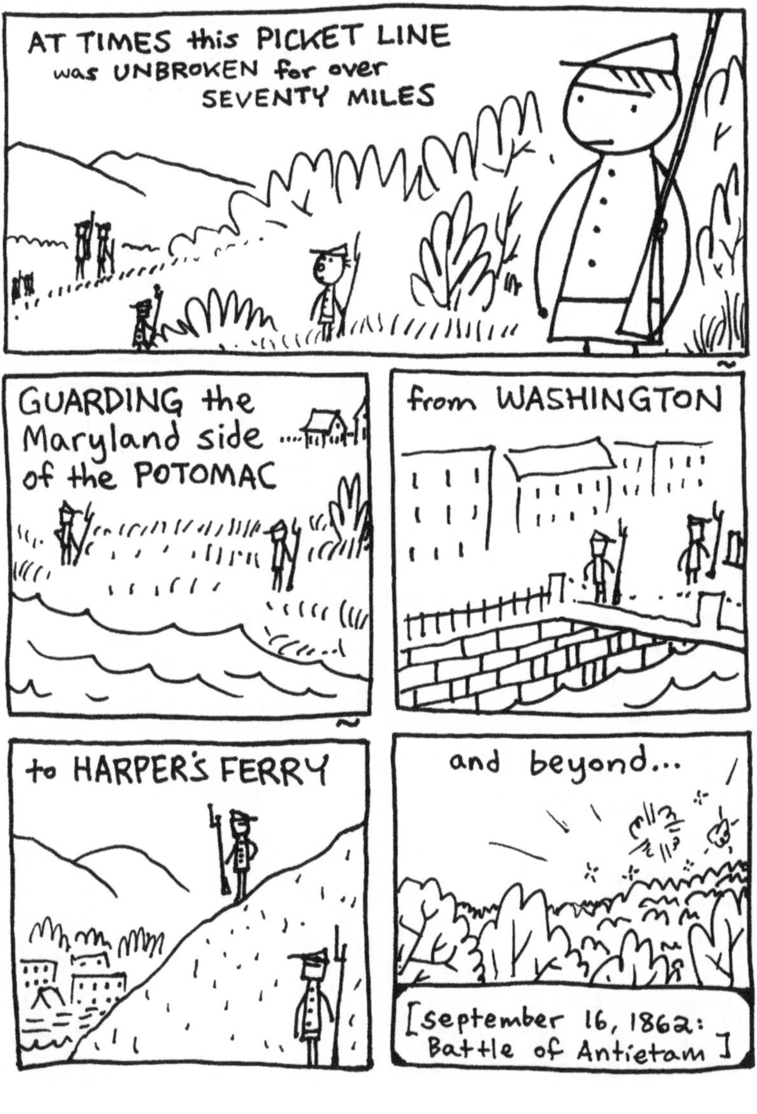
AT TIMES this PICKET LINE was UNBROKEN for over SEVENTY MILES
GUARDING the Maryland side of the POTOMAC
from WASHINGTON
to HARPER'S FERRY
and beyond...
[september 16, 1862: Battle of Antietam]

# FULL STATEMENT

SOON after we were POSTED

a MOUNTED GUARD arrived from CAMP

with ORDERS for JONAS and I to REPORT AT ONCE to Headquarters.

He CONDUCTED us back to CAMP.

On our ARRIVAL at HEADQUARTERS, we found ALL the Regimental Staff Officers present

as well as...

COLONEL **DAVIS**!

I never saw a more FRIGHTENED MAN than JONAS was.

He THOUGHT we were to be AT LEAST COURTMARTIALLED and SHOT,

but I had NO FEAR of any such PUNISHMENT

as we had done NOTHING to DESERVE it.

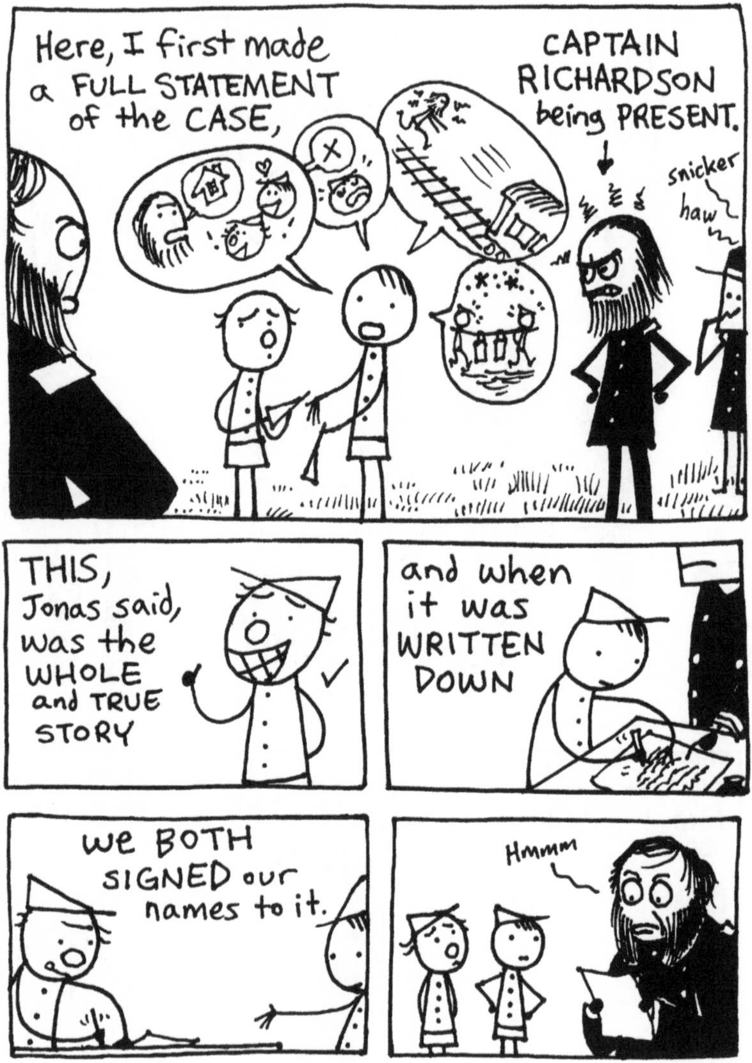
Here, I first made a FULL STATEMENT of the CASE,
CAPTAIN RICHARDSON being PRESENT.
snicker
haw
THIS, Jonas said, was the WHOLE and TRUE STORY
and when it was WRITTEN DOWN
we BOTH SIGNED our names to it.
Hmmm

THAT is a FINE HAND you write, COLBY!

blink blink

And if YOU are the MAN I think you are,

YOU should have a DIFFERENT JOB from CARRYING a MUSKET.

Col. Davis then REPRIMANDED the CAPTAIN

and said WE could PREFER CHARGES against HIM

for NOT GIVING us our RATIONS on the MARCH from ARLINGTON HEIGHTS to POOLVILLE.

He also told the CAPTAIN to: USE them CIVILLY.

I BELIEVE they will be AS GOOD MEN as your WOBURN BOYS.

He CLOSED the HEARING

by sending us WITHOUT GUARDS and ALONE

to our POSTS away on the RIVER

# RETURN TO DUTY

WE RETURNED in a VERY DIFFERENT frame of MIND from when we left them,

and though I KNEW the CAPTAIN would always HATE US

and supposed he would CONTINUE to ABUSE when he could,

with that ONE exception

we received the HEARTY GOODWILL of ALL...

and went AT ONCE ON DUTY with the REST.

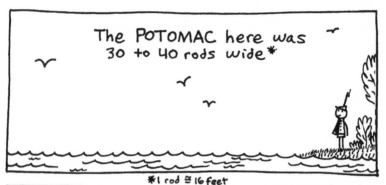

The POTOMAC here was 30 to 40 rods wide*

*1 rod ≅ 16 feet

with SWIFT shallow current

The PICKET LINE was BETWEEN the RIVER and the BALTIMORE & OHIO CANAL→

which was only in USE as far up as EDWARD'S FERRY....

ABOVE US was a NEW YORK REGIMENT.

# THE PICKET LINE

THE LINE consisted of POSTS about 20 RODS* apart.

*20 rods ≅ 320 feet

EACH POST was manned by an OFFICER and FOUR MEN.

~

AT NIGHT, two men PACED the BEATS, ONE on EACH SIDE;

each MARCHING ten rods out, ....

MEETING the man on the NEXT beat

and RETURNING. ....

This they KEPT UP for TWO HOURS

when they were RELIEVED by the other two.

After DAYBREAK only ONE man was kept ON DUTY at a time,

the OTHERS being FREE to REST

or FORAGE for a PIG

or some PEACHES.

This work had been going on ever since the WAR COMMENCED

and was CONTINUED most of that WINTER.

# LOOKOUT

Though the REBELS occupied the VIRGINIA SHORE opposite us

and SMALL PARTIES of them were occasionally SEEN,

NO LARGE FORCE was known to be NEAR

and a VIGILANT LOOKOUT was all that was REQUIRED.

It was our DUTY to give IMMEDIATE NOTICE of any MOVEMENT

and to PREVENT anyone from CROSSING in either direction.

X!

While there was APPARENTLY NO great number of the ENEMY near,

ALARMS were FREQUENT,

and FIVE PRISONERS were taken the VERY FIRST NIGHT we were there.

# BLANKETS

It was most FORTUNATE for us that the WEATHER was MOSTLY FINE

for we had NO SHELTER except our BLANKETS

So we had to MAKE THE MOST of these.

RUBBER BLANKET:
3 feet
6 feet
buttons
button holes

TWO of us

would BUTTON our BLANKETS TOGETHER

and make a TENT out of them,

which was a LITTLE PROTECTION from the heavy AUTUMN DEWS

but NOT very effective in case of a HEAVY STORM.

# ARRIVAL

NEWTON had been LEFT in the FIELD HOSPITAL at ARLINGTON HEIGHTS

but he was ABLE in a day or two to FOLLOW US

RIDING all the way in an AMBULANCE

I soon HEARD of his ARRIVAL

but INSTEAD of being SENT to HIS COMPANY

he was DETAILED with about a DOZEN more MEN

who were SENT to GEORGETOWN

to get the MULES needed for the regiment's BAGGAGE WAGONS.

# GEORGETOWN MULES

It was a TWO DAY TRIP each way.

When they got to the MILITARY DEPOT at Georgetown

there were BUT A FEW MULES LEFT in the STOCKADE set apart for them

and THOSE were as VICIOUS LOOKING BRUTES as one would CARE to SEE,

because the REGIMENTS which had ALREADY DRAWN their MULES

had, of course, SELECTED all the BEST ones.

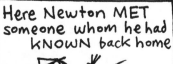 Here Newton MET someone whom he had KNOWN back home

 and STOOD by the fence TALKING with him

while the eleven OTHERS PICKED OUT their MULES;

So HE was the LAST to go after one.

With the HELP of a NEGRO

he FINALLY CAUGHT one

though with a GREAT deal of DIFFICULTY

With a HUNDRED FEET of ROPE

attached to a FRIGHTENED and very LIVELY MULE

he STARTED BACK along the TOW PATH after the rest.

The TOW PATH was ON TOP of the CANAL BANK;

STEEP on both SIDES and VERY ROUGH.

THE MULE was SO STRONG

and set SO SWIFT a pace

that he soon commenced to PAY OUT the ROPE.

Just then he OVERTOOK the OTHER boys PLODDING ALONG with THEIR mules.

VEERING to one side

his own FRIGHTENED BEAST passed them

and GALLOPED on ahead.

They CALLED to him not to LET OUT the ROPE

but he COULDN'T HELP IT and in a FEW MINUTES it was ALL OUT.

The END of the rope was TIED around his WAIST

So it was IMPOSSIBLE to let the MULE go LOOSE.

at that INSTANT his foot SLIPPED

and being a little OUT OF the PATH

he LOST his FOOTING entirely

and went SLIDING and BOUNDING

until he BROUGHT UP with a THUD

The next he KNEW

one of the BOYS was POURING WATER on his FACE.

When his SENSES had fully RETURNED

they ASKED him how it HAPPENED,

WHAT had BECOME of the MULE, &c.

As soon as he was ABLE he WENT ALONG with the rest

and a COUPLE OF MILES farther ON
.......

they found the MULE CALMLY FEEDING beside the path.

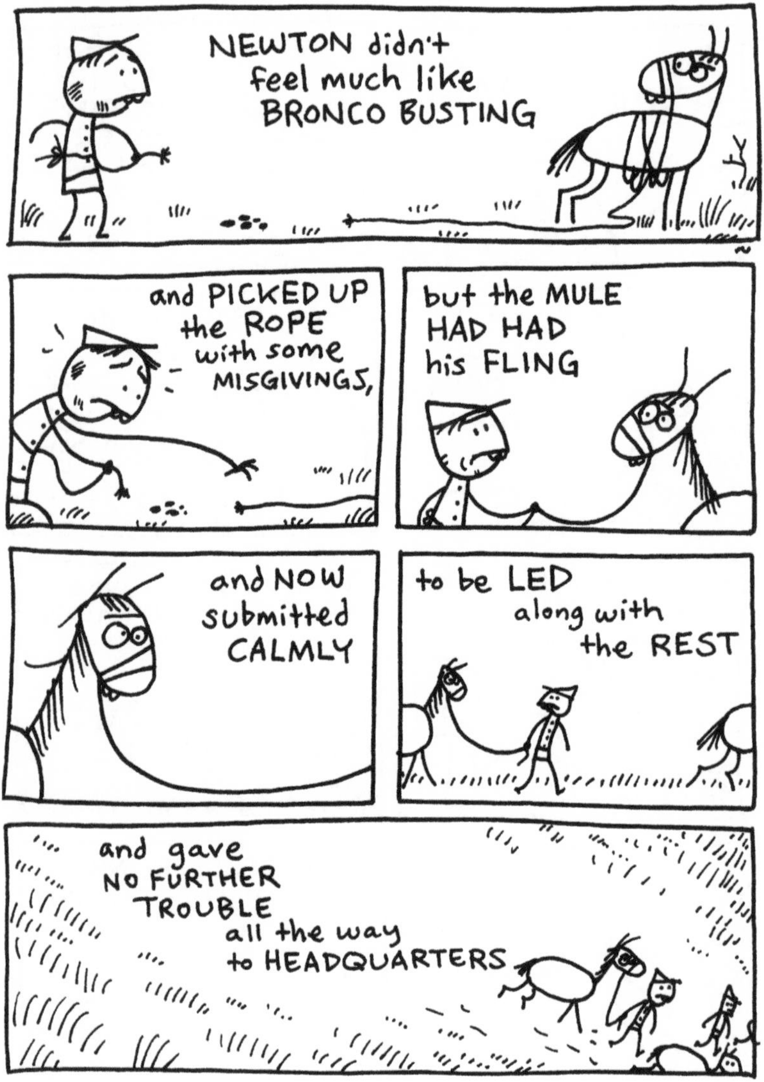
NEWTON didn't feel much like BRONCO BUSTING
and PICKED UP the ROPE with some MISGIVINGS,
but the MULE HAD HAD his FLING
and NOW submitted CALMLY
to be LED along with the REST
and gave NO FURTHER TROUBLE all the way to HEADQUARTERS

They got BACK TO CAMP the 22nd

On the MORNING of the 27th I went to CAMP to SEE HIM.

He was NOT doing FULL DUTY

and only DRILLED with the OTHERS when he FELT like it.

He seemed to ME to be GETTING ALONG all right

and was ENJOYING himself HUGELY.

He told me about seeing some of the BOYS of the 11th NH, and of his TRIP to GEORGETOWN.

I LEFT him about TEN O'CLOCK

and went BACK UP the RIVER

much REASSURED about him.

# AS LIGHT OF IT AS POSSIBLE

:::: But the NEXT MORNING was very HOT

and he was TAKEN suddenly SICK while on GUARD DUTY.

Two men HELPED him get to the SURGEON

who pronounced it a LIGHT SUNSTROKE

and ordered him to the SICK TENT.

Later in the day the COMPANY cook came up to TELL ME about it.

He was soon ABOUT AGAIN

so we made as LIGHT of it as possible when WRITING HOME,

and though he SLEPT about ALL THE TIME

and occasionally seemed to REGAIN his GOOD SPIRITS, for a while,

he was NEVER on ACTIVE DUTY again.

# BALL'S BLUFF

On the 21st of September the year before, the battle of **BALL'S BLUFF** was FOUGHT ALMOST OPPOSITE where COMPANY K was on DUTY.

An IMPRUDENT CROSSING of the river

by a DETACHMENT of UNION TROOPS

resulted in their BEING SURPRISED by a SUPERIOR FORCE.

Instead of
RECROSSING
as quickly as possible,

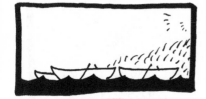

an EFFORT was made
to REINFORCE them.

They were
DRIVEN
to the BOATS

and MANY
were SHOT
from the HIGH BANK

while
ROWING

or
SWIMMING

back to the
MARYLAND
side.

A CANAL BOAT loaded mostly with WOUNDED

was so RIDDLED with BULLETS fired from the BLUFF

that it SUNK with ALL ON BOARD.

Some of our men made FINGER RINGS

out of the BONES they found

that had been WASHED UP by the CURRENT

# ALARM

Although NO DANGER seemed to THREATEN just then,

it was IMPOSSIBLE to say what MIGHT HAPPEN at any time

and hardly a day PASSED without an ALARM of some sort.

SEVERAL of these happened AT NIGHT

and EACH TIME the men OFF DUTY were ORDERED

to PREPARE for MARCH at an INSTANT'S NOTICE.

As a rule, NOTHING MORE was heard

and after a TIME we were ALLOWED to BUNK DOWN again

and TRY to SLEEP.

# FOR EXAMPLE

One of these ALARMS

came at a QUARTER of TEN on the evening of OCTOBER 5th

when WORD was PASSED ALONG

from POST to POST

that there was a SQUAD of REBELS

on the OTHER SIDE of the river...

We were ORDERED to PACK UP

sling our KNAPSACKS

and FALL IN LINE

READY TO MARCH on the INSTANT...

It took but a LITTLE TIME to PACK our FEW belongings

and ASSEMBLE at the post, READY to START at the WORD.

*The* CIVIL WAR DIARY *of* FREEMAN COLBY | **97**

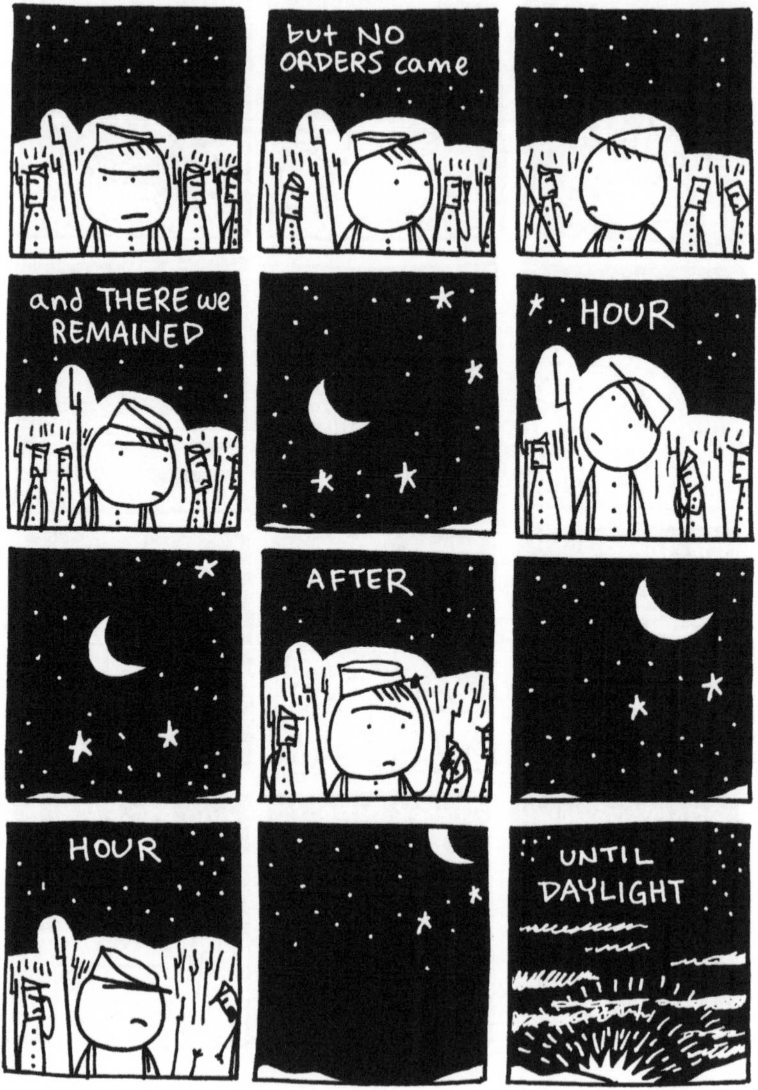
but NO ORDERS came
and THERE we REMAINED
HOUR
AFTER
HOUR
UNTIL DAYLIGHT

when SIGNAL ROCKETS were THROWN UP

from SUGAR MOUNTAIN

and from the ADJOINING CAMPS

and we again had the PRIVILEGE

of UNSLINGING our KNAPSACKS

and getting a little REST.

With DAYLIGHT, NEWS came

that there HAD BEEN an ENGAGEMENT the day before

up the river at HARPER'S FERRY

where OUR TROOPS had CAPTURED a few stands of ARMS

and a LOT of ARMY STORES

which they had SENT down the river to a point of SAFETY.

I DON'T BELIEVE there was a LIVE JOHNNY anywhere NEAR US.

The ALARM and our NIGHT VIGIL

Was ALL a part of the OFFICERS' PLANS to DISCIPLINE US

and I RESOLVED NEVER to be FRIGHTENED at any such DEMONSTRATION

until the BULLETS WHISTLED.

NEXT DAY we were ORDERED BACK to camp.

# CAMP LIFE

THE CAMP was in a fine GROVE of WHITE OAK

where the ROAD to CONRAD'S FERRY branched off.

Poolville
Edwards Ferry
Conrads Ferry

The POTOMAC was less than a MILE away.

Just opposite us was another LOW HILL on the VIRGINIA side

while FARTHER UP was BALL'S BLUFF and SUGAR MOUNTAIN.

Across the ROAD from us was a BATTERY of 12 GUNS.

NONE of us were any too well PLEASED with the CHANGE to the monotonous GRIND of CAMP LIFE

after the COMPARATIVE FREEDOM of the PICKET LINE,

where we had been ABLE to FORAGE at will,

Cook our own MEALS,

and DO about AS WE LIKED

as long as we were ON HAND to STAND GUARD in our TURN.

*The* CIVIL WAR DIARY *of* FREEMAN COLBY | 101

# A REGULAR DAY'S WORK IN CAMP:

ROLL CALL at 5-30

BREAKFAST at 6

(made by the COMPANY COOK in camp)

SQUAD DRILL 6-30 to 7-30

COMPANY DRILL from 10 to 11

DINNER at 12

BATTALION DRILL from 3 to 5

DRESS PARADE at 5-30

SUPPER at 6-30

ROLL CALL at 8-30

TAPS at 9

when ALL LIGHTS must be PUT OUT.

## DETAILS

A DETAIL of about 60 MEN was made each day

for POLICE DUTY

(SWEEPING and CLEANING camp)

and GUARD DUTY

and every few days as many as 50 MEN

with HALF that number of AXES

were sent INTO THE WOODS to work up WOOD

and BRING IT BACK on the WAGONS

for the COMPANY COOKS

and OFFICERS' QUARTERS.

# AXES

The AXES were of the USUAL KIND used in the SOUTH

(Double-Bitted!)

but QUITE STRANGE to us NORTHERNERS.

I have often WATCHED the BLACKS...

TURNING the axe at EACH STROKE

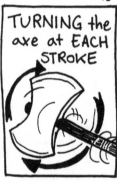

so as to GIVE A BLOW first with ONE BLADE

and THEN with the OTHER

OUR WOOD was cut about FOUR FEET LONG and SPLIT FINE.

It was SURPRISING to see HOW MUCH would be WORKED UP in a little time

by a SQUAD of GREEN MEN.

# TEAM WORK

I had a CHUM named PETER WARREN, a fine ROBUST fellow

(a CARPENTER by TRADE)

When we were TOGETHER on one of these WOOD DETAILS

by TAKING TURNS with the AXE

we CUT DOWN a YELLOW OAK tree 14 INCHES THROUGH

in a SINGLE DAY

and were ALL READY to Go back to CAMP with the REST at 4-30.

EUCHRE was our FAVORITE game

and the ONLY INTERRUPTIONS

were when the CORPORAL came around.

Then ONE of us WOULD STRIKE a few BLOWS,

take out a FRESH CHIP or two

and SETTLE BACK to PLAY again

as he disappeared in the DIRECTION of the NEXT group of WORKERS.

As a SHARP AXE was UNKNOWN

and FEW of the MEN had EVER handled one before,

PETER and I could do QUITE AS MUCH

as the NEXT pair

and STILL have TIME for up to A HUNDRED GAMES at a sitting.

# TARGET PRACTICE

My FIRST DETAIL after our return to CAMP

was for NIGHT GUARD duty.

WHEN we were RELIEVED in the MORNING

We FIRED OFF our GUNS at a TARGET.

THOSE making the POOREST SHOTS

were put at the HEAD of the LIST

for SUCH DUTY,

thus making GOOD MARKSMANSHIP quite an object.

THIS was the FIRST TIME I had ever had a chance to FIRE my MUSKET

but I made a FAIR SHOT

though not NEARLY SO GOOD as some of the OTHERS.

THEY had FIRED THEIRS EVERY TIME they had been on DUTY...

and they had in FRESH CHARGES

while MY CHARGE was RUSTED into the GUN,

making it KICK BADLY.

It also PULLED OFF much TOO HARD.

 ALTHOUGH it was STRICTLY FORBIDDEN to TAMPER in any way with one's GUN,

I took the FIRST OPPORTUNITY

 of BORROWING a FILE of the BLACKSMITH

and after HUNTING UP a SPOT where I was NOT LIKELY to be SEEN

 I TOOK OFF the LOCK and FILED the TRIGGER NOTCH

UNTIL the TRIGGER would PULL to suit me.

AFTER THAT I was able to make a BULLSEYE almost every time it came my TURN to SHOOT,

 EARNING ME FREEDOM from night guard DUTY for WEEKS at a time.

CAMP STORIES

REPORTS were now CURRENT

that an ARMISTICE for 60 or 90 DAYS
....

was being ARRANGED

CSA    USA

but for what PURPOSE we did NOT know

and though RUMORS were IN THE AIR for SEVERAL DAYS,

in the END, NOTHING AT ALL came of it.

This was like MANY other CAMP STORIES that were in CIRCULATION all the time;

they were BEYOND ANYTHING you can IMAGINE.

NEW RUMORS were heard EVERY hour in the day

and not ONE in TEN of them had a PARTICLE of FOUNDATION

EXCEPT in the FERTILE BRAIN of some LAZY PRIVATE

who wanted to GET UP a little SENSATION.

REAL NEWS was SCARCE indeed

and NOTHING could be DEPENDED UPON

UNLESS it came from a STAFF OFFICER

OR was seen in a NORTHERN newspaper.

# NEWSPAPERS

These were about as RELIABLE as they ARE at PRESENT

and CONTRADICTED in EACH ISSUE

MUCH of what they had PRINTED as NEWS the DAY or WEEK before.

NEVERTHELESS, we thought ALMOST AS MUCH of them as of the HOME LETTERS

and when a BUNDLE of them was RECEIVED by one of the BOYS

it was READ and RE-READ

and PASSED from HAND to HAND

until they were WORN OUT.

# PEACHES

For several evenings an old COLORED MAN peddled

PEACHES!

in the CAMP,

moving from GROUP to GROUP of the SOLDIERS

OFFERING his FRUIT for sale.

We WONDERED where he GOT them

but NO ONE seemed to kNOW

until ONE DAY I WATCHED him

and FOUND that he was STEALING THEM from his MASTER'S GARDEN

and HIDING them in a STRAW STACK

UNTIL he should GET a CHANCE to take them TO CAMP.

WHILE he was GONE for another LOAD

I TIED a string around EACH SLEEVE of my BLOUSE

and managed to CONFISCATE and REMOVE what HE had GATHERED —

about THREE PECKS

into the EDGE of a CORNFIELD CLOSE BY.

You should have SEEN that N*****R when he FOUND they were GONE!

# HOSPITALITY

The RULE against FORAGING was very STRICT

X!

but it was IMPOSSIBLE to PREVENT the boys from doing a LITTLE of it ~

and it was on such EXPEDITIONS

that we could SEE THE PEOPLE as they REALLY lived.

In SPITE of the STRONG REBEL SENTIMENTS of the residents in general

We occasionally met with GOOD UNION PEOPLE in UNEXPECTED places,

while OTHERS who were frankly CONFEDERATE in sympathy

yet showed towards US the SPIRIT of true SOUTHERN HOSPITALITY.

# CAUGHT AT IT

One day **NEWTON** and CHARLIE HART got the AFTERNOON OFF

and HAVING HEARD there was a fine PEACH ORCHARD a few miles from camp,

they thought THAT would be a GOOD CHANCE to have a FEAST.

They STARTED OFF across COUNTRY

and after a LONG WALK

they reached the ORCHARD...

They got OVER the FENCE

and EACH ONE CLIMBED a tree.

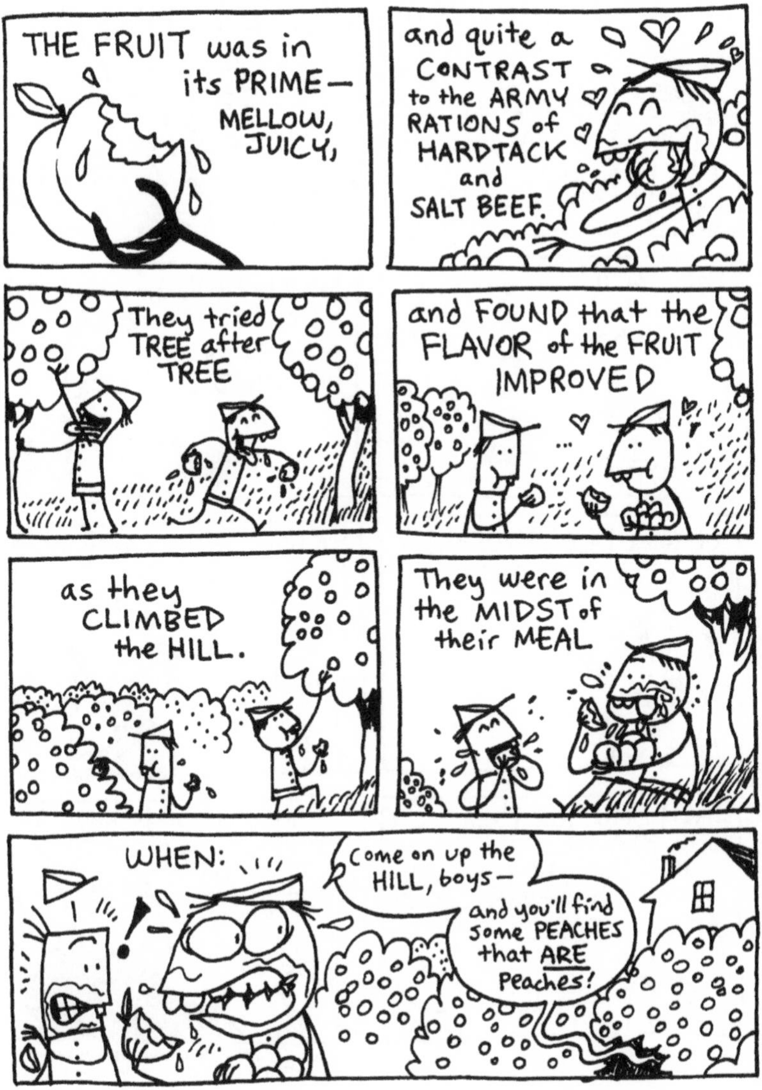
THE FRUIT was in its PRIME— MELLOW, JUICY,
and quite a CONTRAST to the ARMY RATIONS of HARDTACK and SALT BEEF.
They tried TREE after TREE
and FOUND that the FLAVOR of the FRUIT IMPROVED
as they CLIMBED the HILL.
They were in the MIDST of their MEAL
WHEN:
Come on up the HILL, boys—
and you'll find some PEACHES that ARE Peaches!

They were ASHAMED at being CAUGHT at it,

but WHAT could they DO?

They didn't care to RUN AWAY so they FOLLOWED the FARMER

WONDERING, meanwhile whether he MEANT to be KIND

or was LEADING them into a TRAP.

He took them from TREE to TREE

EACH ONE laden with PEACHES FINER than they had EVER TASTED...

And now boys, how about some SUPPER? *

*Transcript illegible here, but the farmer definitely invites them to his house.

They TRIED to ESCAPE the INVITATION

but he would accept NO EXCUSES

so they WENT ALONG with him to the HOUSE.

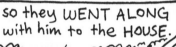

AT SUPPER, there were more PEACHES in HUGE yellow BOWLS

with PLENTY of CORN PONE and rich MILK.

He knew the WAY to their HEARTs all right

urpf

and when AFTER supper was OVER they HURRIED AWAY to CAMP

he CALLED after them,

COME AGAIN, boys, and have some MORE PEACHES!

# FARMLAND

Most of the country we could see was CLEARED and in GRASS or CROPS of some kind.

The LITTLE WOODS were on the TOPS of the HILLS and along the STREAMS.

It was mostly OAK, with scattered HICKORY and BUTTONWOOD.

The rest of the land, being SMOOTH and FREE from ROCKS,

was EASY to WORK even on the HILLSIDES.

There were but FEW POTATOES — I never saw more than HALF AN ACRE of them...

There were occasional fields of TOBACCO of 3 or 4 acres...

CROPS

On most of the TILLAGE LAND, THREE CROPS followed each other in ROTATION: CORN, WHEAT, and GRASS.

Last year's WHEAT GROUND was SOWN to GRASS

and turned into PASTURE.

Little HAY was cut as the STOCK stayed OUT OF DOORS and GRAZED most of the winter.

This crop of grass was followed the NEXT YEAR with CORN.

At that time the CORN was just being SHOCKED,

though some farmers ONLY broke off the EARS,

and left the FODDER for CATTLE to BROWSE on during COLD WEATHER.

It took a team of THREE HORSES to LOOSEN the ground

So that the FALL RAINS would SOAK IN instead of RUNNING OFF

for the ground, being mostly CLAY, was BAKED HARD by the summer heat.

After PLOUGHING, WHEAT was DRILLED IN...

At HARVEST TIME, this was STACKED right in the field.

# HOUSING

As the farms were LARGE, there were but few GOOD HOUSES to be seen...

The HUTS of the NEGROES were usually at the back

but a few were to be seen along the ROADS...

Poor, shiftless looking SHANTIES, most of them...

The FENCES were of HICKORY, and would last a LIFETIME.

# SHORT RATIONS

For the first few WEEKS we were at EDWARD'S FERRY

our RATIONS were occasionally a bit SHORT

but after a while the COLONEL seemed to THINK

the QUARTERMASTER could do BETTER by us

and GAVE HIM a good TALKING TO.

Some of the boys THOUGHT there MUST have been a BIG PROFIT in the SUPPLY CONTRACTS

but HOWEVER that may be, we NOW had a PLENTY to EAT

and SELDOM afterwards SUFFERED from a SCARCITY of food

though SOMETIMES the QUALITY was NONE TOO GOOD.

# ANOTHER EXCURSION

On Saturday, OCTOBER 16

the REBELS CROSSED the Potomac

on BOTH SIDES of us

and DROVE the 10th VERMONT

which was NEXT BELOW US

back AWAY from the river

That night we SLEPT with our GUNS for PILLOWS

and SUNDAY MORNING after an INSPECTION of ARMS

we STARTED about half past eleven for CONRAD'S FERRY

We were LOADED with EVERYTHING we had

and it was SIX MILES to Conrad's Ferry.

When we GOT THERE we learned

that there HAD BEEN a SKIRMISH earlier in the day

TWO MILES farther on

but it was ALL OVER by that time.

The JOHNNIES had succeeded in TAKING a few of our CAVALRYMEN prisoners

but were DRIVEN BACK across the river by some PENNSYLVANIA troops before we got there

so all there was for US to do was to GO BACK.

126 | MAREK BENNETT

A good nice steady RAIN fell as we MARCHED

and as we TRAMPED along in the DRIZZLE

we were DISPOSED to think this ANOTHER EXCURSION

got up by the OFFICERS for the sake of DISCIPLINE

and to give US a little WORK to do

but as the PICKETS were TAKEN IN as we went along

leaving the river BARE

we CONCLUDED that there was MORE to it AFTER ALL...

but what it MIGHT BE we had NO MEANS of KNOWING.

....

# MUDDY BRANCH

A few days later we MOVED to a new CAMPING PLACE

on a CREEK called: the Muddy Branch

Like most Southern streams it FLOWED in a NARROW CHANNEL between STEEP BANKS of red clay.

The CURRENT was SLUGGISH but it furnished our ONLY water supply,

being BROUGHT in PAILS up a STEEP PATH from the stream

to the LEVEL FIELD above

We were HARDLY settled in

when on OCTOBER 11th Colonel Davis received MARCHING ORDERS for the regiment.

# MARCHING ORDERS?

We were NOTIFIED to be PREPARED to LEAVE at ANY TIME,

the delivery of MAIL was STOPPED;

MANY of the DRILLS and other ROUTINE WORK DISCONTINUED,

and an AIR of EXPECTANCY was noticeable on ALL SIDES.

THINKING as we did that a GENERAL MOVEMENT of the FIELD FORCES was in progress

and knowing the GOOD REPUTATION borne by MASSACHUSETTS TROOPS....

We LOOKED FORWARD to ACTIVE SERVICE in the near future

and were CONFIDENT of being ABLE to do our part.

BUT day after day PASSED

and STILL we WAITED for the order

to BREAK CAMP and take to the ROAD.

NOTHING MORE was heard until OCTOBER 17th —

when our MARCHING ORDERS were COUNTERMANDED,

never mind

leaving us to SETTLE DOWN once more to the USUAL ROUTINE.

zzzz

Most of the BOYS preferred ANY change

to the MONOTONY of camp life

and GUARD DUTY

but their DISAPPOINTMENT at REMAINING

was tempered with REJOICING

over the delivery of the ACCUMULATED MAIL.

MAIL

# MAIL

MAIL was supposed to be SENT and RECEIVED on TUESDAYS and FRIDAYS,

being carried to and from WASHINGTON by SPECIAL MESSENGER

But the TIME of their trips was very ELASTIC

as they were made to suit the CONVENIENCE of the OFFICERS.

TROOPS under MARCHING ORDERS got NO MAIL

so when our orders were COUNTERMANDED

ALL the MAIL that had COME IN since the LAST DELIVERY, October 8th,

was DISTRIBUTED AT ONCE.

We were MORE GLAD than I can say

to hear from HOME again.

I had a BIG LETTER from MOTHER, FATHER, and the GIRLS

and one each from UNCLE HENRY PIPER, ROBERT HARRIMAN, and GEORGE D. COLBY

EACH ONE wanted to know what WE thought of the WAR

as WE SAW IT at the FRONT,

WHAT the PROSPECT of its SOON coming to an END,

what I thought of the SLAVES

and lots of OTHER questions.

FATHER was SO ENTHUSIASTIC that despite his 48 YEARS he talked SERIOUSLY of ENLISTING.

There was NOT TIME to answer them ALL at once

SO I REPLIED to the HOME letter FIRST,

telling FATHER that we had NOT begun to FIGHT yet,

that it needed BETTER TEETH than HIS to chew HARDTACK

and that ALL his WORK was needed at HOME to TAKE CARE of MOTHER and ELLEN and EMMA.

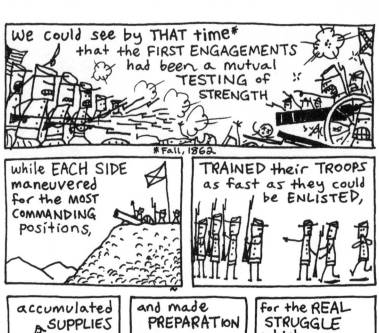

We could see by THAT time* that the FIRST ENGAGEMENTS had been a mutual TESTING of STRENGTH

*Fall, 1862

while EACH SIDE maneuvered for the MOST COMMANDING positions,

TRAINED their TROOPS as fast as they could be ENLISTED,

accumulated SUPPLIES

and made PREPARATION in every possible way

for the REAL STRUGGLE which was yet to COME.

I ventured to PREDICT...that it would take ALL of THREE YEARS to END the war,

and that to keep OUR troops GUARDING REBEL PROPERTY,

was NOT by any means the WAY to go about it.

# FORAGING

| | | |
|---|---|---|
| ALTHOUGH the people near us were all REBELS  | their PROPERTY was PROTECTED,  | NO FORAGING was allowed,  |
| and WE were not allowed to USE so much as a FENCE RAIL  | or an ARMFUL of STRAW  | without PAYING for it.  |
| After we MOVED into the NEW CAMP  | some of the men went out to an OLD STACK  | and GOT some STRAW for BEDDING.  |
| NEXT MORNING the Colonel PAID for it,  | put a GUARD over the STACK  | and NOTIFIED us that the AMOUNT would be TAKEN OUT of OUR PAY.  |

About the same time, some of the BOYS, while on PICKET,

captured FIVE PIGS.

The owner SWORE there were 27 of them

and the COLONEL PAID him $150 for them,

taxing the PRIVATES again for this.

These SUMS were never ACTUALLY taken out of our PAY,

but many of the boys BELIEVED they WOULD be, and RESENTED it accordingly.

The FARMERS about there

TOLD US that the REBELS

were JUST AS GOOD as the UNION soldiers

and then our OFFICERS would go and TAKE DINNER with them

and SET the PRIVATES to GUARD their PROPERTY.

Even the NEGROES seemed to LOOK DOWN on a MAN from the NORTH

though the OFFICERS from the COLONEL

down to the LIEUTENANTS of companies

had EACH from ONE to SIX NEGROES for SERVANTS

and THEY were FED BETTER

RIGHT before our EYES

than WE were,

and at the GOVERNMENT'S EXPENSE.

# RANK

MANY of the OFFICERS had been GIVEN their RANK through their INFLUENTIAL friends or relatives.

SOME of them were mere BOYS.

Others, though OLDER,

were NOT FIT to be in COMMAND of a PAIR of MULES.

But EACH ONE must be SALUTED and ADDRESSED just the same.

It was HARD for MANY of US who had been BROUGHT UP to CONSIDER ourselves as GOOD as the NEXT MAN

to do THIS,

ESPECIALLY when some CHESTY young LIEUTENANT just out of SCHOOL

made the ROUND of the CAMP

THREE or FOUR times a DAY

MERELY to see US PRIVATES get up and SALUTE as he PASSED.

We were RESTIVE too

at the INACTION.

WE thought the way to END the WAR was to USE what REBEL PROPERTY we could

instead of STANDING GUARD over it,

and that there were ENOUGH UNION TROOPS within 25 miles

to ADVANCE our line ACROSS the POTOMAC

and PUSH ON to RICHMOND

without a COUNTERMARCH.

The ADMINISTRATION at Washington came in for CRITICISM,

but most of it was DIRECTED at the OFFICERS.

A few HOTHEADS even made THREATS of what would HAPPEN to some of them

IF we should ever get into a BATTLE.

# RAIN

We got an idea when we FIRST went out there — that it only RAINED four or five times a YEAR,

but NOW we commenced to LEARN by hard experience how MISTAKEN that was.

In LATE OCTOBER a COLD RAIN commenced which lasted for THREE DAYS.

at the SAME TIME the WIND blew SO HARD

that from ONE to HALF a DOZEN of our SIBLEY TENTS would be DOWN at a time.

Of course WE would be DRENCHED THROUGH before they could be RIGHTED and PEGGED DOWN again.

The GROUND got SOFT.

Yes, VERY soft —

SO SOFT we had to go HALF WAY to our KNEES in MUD

to get a cup of WATER from the CREEK

which NOW ran FLOOD-HIGH

almost FELLING its BANKS.

And it is SOLID TRUTH that THAT CUP of water, when SETTLED,

would have THREE-EIGHTHS of an INCH of PURE RED MARYLAND MUD in the BOTTOM.

For ONCE, the stream LIVED UP well to its name: Muddy BRANCH

The RAIN STOPPED at last

but the WIND continued to BLOW very HARD

and in time the MUD dried and HARDENED

So we could WALK ABOUT on TOP of it.

But the CREEK still POURED its red-brown FLOOD past us,

HEAVY with the upland clay—

and WE had to WASH with it

COOK with it,

and DRINK it.

The RESULT was that about EVERY OTHER man in the REGIMENT

SOON had a touch of JAUNDICE, MALARIA, or BOWEL TROUBLE.

SOME CASES kept the SURGEON VERY BUSY for a while.

# SICK-CALL

JONAS soon developed the unmistakable SYMPTOMS of JAUNDICE.

The rest of us JOKED him about his COMPLEXION

←(yellow)

but HE failed to RESPOND with his usual LIGHT-HEARTEDNESS . . . . . . . .

and INDEED, he was NOT to be BLAMED for he was SICK ENOUGH

and it was HARDLY a JOKE to be SICK under those circumstances.

The GENERAL HEALTH of the Regiment had averaged VERY GOOD ever since we came out.

Now the SICK-CALL brought quite a LINE OF MEN to file by the SURGEON'S TENT for TREATMENT

but MANY of them merely wanted to get EXCUSED from DUTY

# TREATMENT

So the SURGEON was always on the LOOKOUT for MEN trying to PLAY SICK

to GET OUT of WORKING

and considered himself an EXPERT at DISCOVERING and FOILING them.

His REGULAR TREATMENT of REAL ailments was said to be quite SUFFICIENT

to DISCOURAGE ANYONE from applying to HIM for relief unless it was absolutely NECESSARY,

for he DEALT OUT CASTOR OIL, SALTS, and CALOMEL with an UNSPARING hand.

If THESE were POTENT to CURE our ILLS,

there was LITTLE NEED of REMAINING SICK.

I had enjoyed the BEST OF HEALTH all the time.

The OPEN AIR LIFE agreed with me and my WEIGHT had gone UP to 148 (5 pounds more than ever before).

I had NEVER reported SICK or FALLEN OUT on a MARCH

(and this LAST was something FEW could say).

But a FEW DAYS after the BIG RAIN, I got up one morning VERY SICK

and much as I DISLIKED to do so, I had to go to the DOCTOR.

HE told me it was ONLY A COLD,

gave me some CASTOR OIL and a dose of QUININE

and put me DOWN FOR DUTY

The NEXT day I was WORSE

and he added some COUGH DROPS.

A little later I was put on a DETAIL

but I was TOO SICK to work

and went to the CAPTAIN to get EXCUSED.

He said: NO.

but I told him I should NOT do DUTY for I was not ABLE.

As HE still insisted that AS the SURGEON had NOT marked me for QUARTERS or put me in the HOSPITAL TENT

I was ALL RIGHT for DUTY.

HE had already PUT ME on EXTRA DUTY twice

to SPARE his WOBURN friends

So I HAD TO STAND UP for myself

and TELL him he could PUT me in the GUARDHOUSE,

take me BEFORE the COLONEL,

or anything ELSE he chose,

BUT that he would NEVER be able to PLAY PARTIALITY on ME

because I was a NEW HAMPSHIRE MAN

instead of a NATIVE of NORTH WOBURN

By THAT time he was getting HOT and PUFFY

but in TRYING to MAKE ME COMPLY

he tried to SCARE me to it

by THREATENING to WITHOLD the THREE MONTHS PAY DUE me

UNLESS I DID DUTY that day.

I went to my TENT

Caring little WHAT became of me

for I was TOO SICK to MIND

but I THOUGHT I would GET my PAY about the SAME TIME the rest got THEIRS.

IF I DIDN'T, I vowed WOE BE TO the Captain

IF we should ever BOTH get back to Massachusetts again.

When I AWOKE the next morning, October 29,

I could NOT get to my FEET

until I first CRAWLED up

and STOOD awhile on my HANDS and KNEES
....  ........  ....

to EASE the PAIN in my back.

I reported AGAIN at SICK CALL and when my TURN came

I OPENED UP the bosom of my SHIRT...

I think I have the "Yallers."

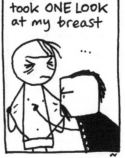
The SURGEON took ONE LOOK at my breast ...

and IMMEDIATELY pronounced it a case of:

Jaundice!

He gave me a BLUE PILL to take AT ONCE

and AT NIGHT a dose of SALTS to carry it off,

and for TEN DAYS I had my BLUE PILL every morning

and DOSE of SALTS at night.

He gave me some more QUININE, too.

I took it faithfully

until my HEAD BUZZED

then kept the REST in my POCKET

UNTIL, finding it was doing me NO GOOD there,

I threw it away.

HOSPITAL

Of course, NEWTON and JONAS were having ALL they could ATTEND TO to look after THEMSELVES,

So I had to GO to the HOSPITAL TENT.

HOSPITAL →

Even THERE the CARE was NONE TOO GOOD

for CONVALESCENTS were made to DO DUTY as NURSES

sniff    sniff

for those who were TOO SICK to MOVE about.

Cough sniffle cough    cough    cough    Cough. Cough. COUGH. hack!

sniff    ooooog    sniff

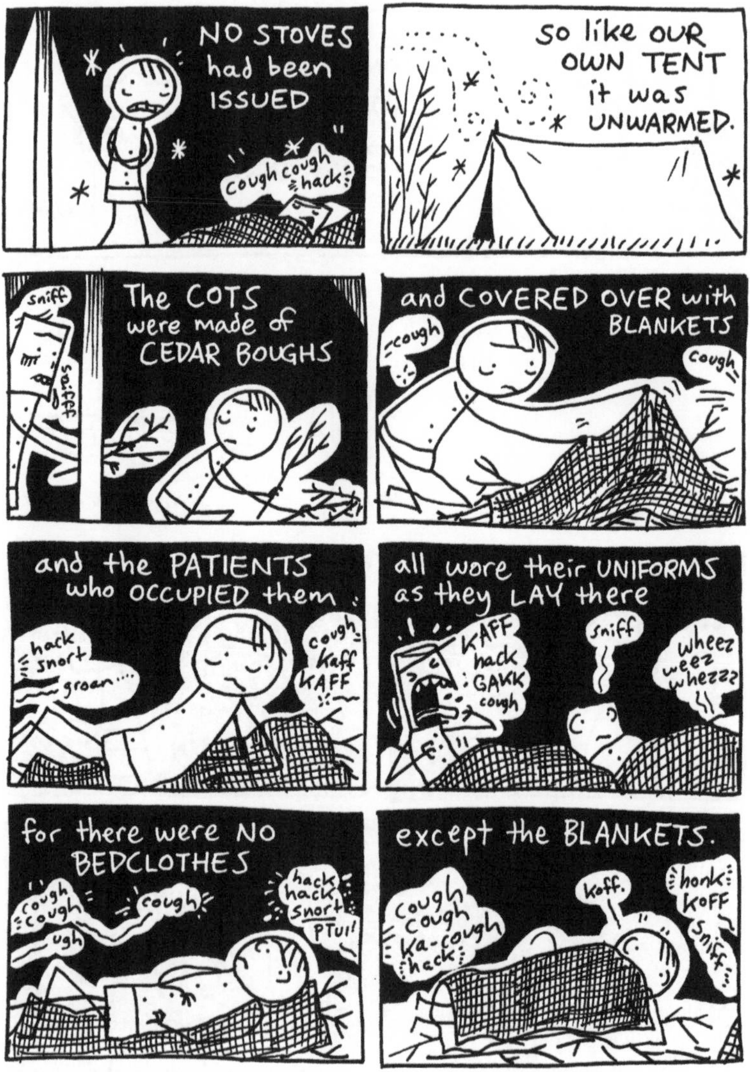
NO STOVES had been ISSUED
cough cough hack
so like OUR OWN TENT it was UNWARMED.
sniff
The COTS were made of CEDAR BOUGHS
and COVERED OVER with BLANKETS
cough
cough
and the PATIENTS who OCCUPIED them
hack snort groan....
cough kaff KAFF
all wore their UNIFORMS as they LAY there
KAFF hack GAKK cough
sniff
wheez weez whezzz
for there were NO BEDCLOTHES
cough cough
cough
ugh
hack hack snort PTUI!
except the BLANKETS.
cough cough Ka-cough hack
koff.
honk KOFF sniff...

# GRAYBACKS

Before a man was WELL ENOUGH to LEAVE his bunk

ANOTHER would be WAITING to CRAWL INTO IT

and WRAP HIMSELF in the BLANKETS.

In this way the BUNKS were OCCUPIED

by MAN AFTER MAN, in succession;

some of them CLEAN,

others COVERED with DIRT

and — WORSE STILL — with CRAWLING THINGS

which BRED and MULTIPLIED in these CONGENIAL QUARTERS

Until there was NO SPOT in the whole TENT

FREE from them.

We called them GRAYBACKS.

I was presently COVERED with them

and they were SO BIG

I was AFRAID they would CARRY me off—

OR carry off my CLOTHES and LEAVE ME without anything.

They were a TORMENT indeed

for they left me NO PEACE by NIGHT

or DAY

and the THOUGHT of LEAVING them BEHIND offered the GREATEST possible INDUCEMENT to HURRY UP and GET WELL.

# BACK TO QUARTERS

You may be SURE I was GLAD when early in NOVEMBER

the SURGEON allowed me to GO BACK to QUARTERS.

BUT, the GRAYBACKS went along TOO

so the NEXT TASK was to GET RID of THEM.

This was NOT a very PROMISING JOB as ALL I could DO was TAKE my SHIRT OFF each day,

PICK OFF the graybacks and CRACK them.

When THAT was finished, I would PUT IT ON again

and do the SAME THING with my PANTS.

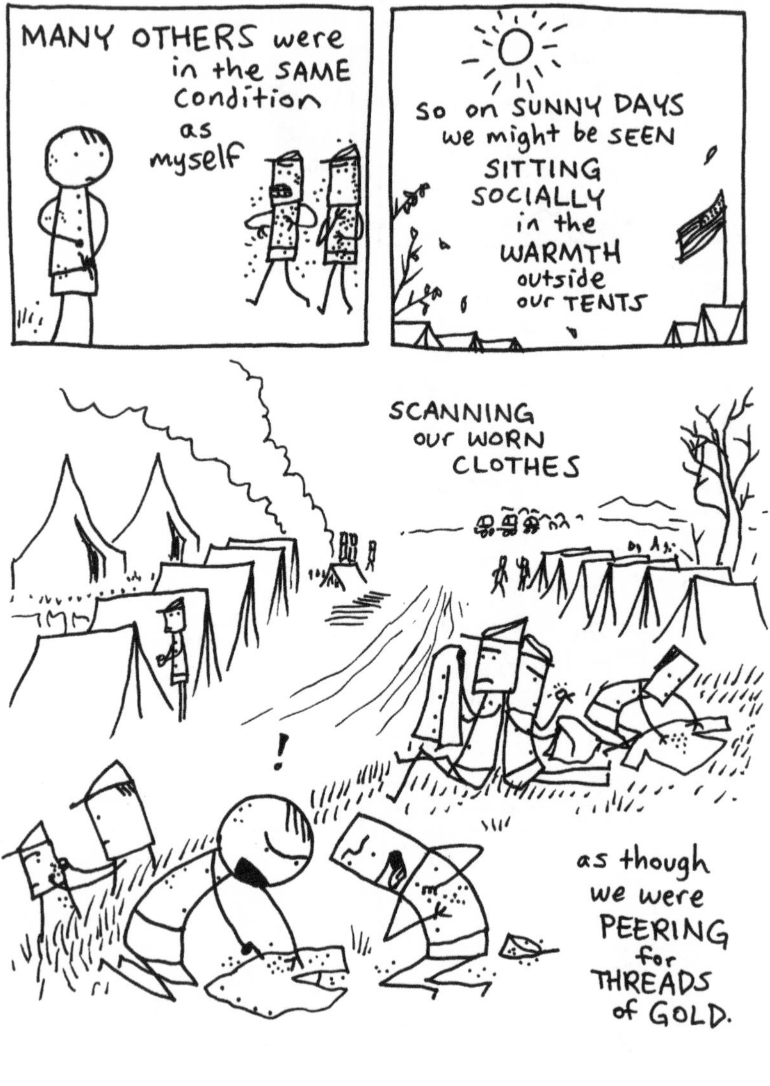
MANY OTHERS were in the SAME condition as myself
So on SUNNY DAYS we might be SEEN SITTING SOCIALLY in the WARMTH outside our TENTS
SCANNING our WORN CLOTHES
!
as though we were PEERING for THREADS of GOLD.

# HARDIHOOD

EACH of our CAMPS in turn, after it had been OCCUPIED a little while

became OVERRUN with these PESTS

and only by CONSTANT INDUSTRY

could they be KEPT DOWN in our TENTS and personal effects.

SOME MEN who took LITTLE PAINS to keep CLEAN

were LOUSY ALL the time they were in the service.

Neither the RIDICULE and SCOFFS of their FELLOWS

or the TONGUE LASHING of the OFFICERS were of the SLIGHTEST effect.

SOMETIMES when one of them was JOKED about it by his COMRADES,

I have seen him IN BRAVADO UNBUTTON the front of his SHIRT

and SHOW a HAIRY FRONT covered with CRAWLING GRAYBACKS

which HE never seemed to MIND in the least,

regarding the MEN who spent SO MUCH TIME and PAINS trying to keep FREE of them

as FINICKY and rather LACKING in the HARDIHOOD of a SOLDIER.

But they drove ME nearly CRAZY

SO AT LAST in desperation I wrote HOME

for a box of "AUNT GUINTUM"

to be SENT me at ONCE BY MAIL.

Father SENT it

but BEFORE it GOT THERE

the SURGEON gave me SOMETHING to put on my CLOTHES

which DROVE THEM nearly all AWAY

and after THAT you may be SURE I tried HARD ENOUGH to keep FREE from them

but NOT ALWAYS with ENTIRE success.

# RATIONS

For SOME TIME after leaving the SICK TENT, my STOMACH craved MORE FOOD

than the ONE SLICE of toasted BREAD for each meal, which was the ALLOWANCE of the PATIENTS there,

BUT it would NOT TAKE CARE of the REGULAR army ration.

This was MOSTLY MADE UP of:

Hardtack / OR boiled "SALT HORSE" (salted beef)

Boiled fresh BEEF

COFFEE

NO PORK was being issued at this time,

NOR any POTATOES or FRESH VEGETABLES of any kind.

BAKED BEANS, stewed beans, or SOUP

were served ONCE A WEEK or so for a CHANGE

BLORPX!

# THE USUAL MEAL

A slice of MEAT about the SIZE of a MAN'S HAND

with HARDTACK

KA-CLUNKA

and a tin dipper of COFFEE.

The HARDTACK was FLOUR and WATER

sploosh

BAKED into CRACKERS

3 INCHES square

½ INCH thick

and SO HARD that ONLY the STRONGEST teeth

could make ANY IMPRESSION at all on it.

Men could do GOOD WORK on these RATIONS when they were WELL,

but it REQUIRED a STRONG DIGESTION to handle it

and THIS we CONVALESCENTS LACKED

So we ALL LONGED for a good HOME-COOKED MEAL.

We TALKED IT OVER together in the TENT and found a COMMON INTEREST

in POTATOES, FRESH vegetables, and soft BREAD.

It seemed to ME that if I could have a FEW MEALS of SUCH FOOD

with a little ROASTED or FRIED MEAT

instead of the ETERNAL BOILED BEEF the Camp cook HANDED OUT to us,

and some nice BISCUITS and PIE and FRESH MILK

that I would be ALL RIGHT AGAIN in a week or so.

# OUR REGIMENTAL SUTLER was named PULLEN.

### HiS STOCK IN TRADE included:

PROVISIONS

CUTLERY

STATIONARY

THREAD, NEEDLES

SHOESTRINGS

SUSPENDERS

and other LIGHT GOODS.

His price for BUTTER was from 40¢ to $1 a POUND.

I bought some a few times

and found it ECONOMICAL even at THAT PRICE.

It was often so OLD and STRONG

that to TASTE it was QUITE UNNECESSARY—

a single SMELL was a GREAT PLENTY.

POTATOES were FOUR to SIX cents a pound,

SWEET POTATOES TEN,

RAISINS thirty,

and TOBACCO a DOLLAR and a QUARTER.

FIGS were TWO CENTS each

APPLES four and LEMONS five— when he HAD them.

But these were STRICTLY CASH prices

and FEW of US by that time had any MONEY left to SPEND.

# PAY

We were SUPPOSED to get $13.00 a month

but NO PAY MASTER had been NEAR us

so the LITTLE CASH we had mostly came from HOME.

When I LEFT THERE I carried MORE MONEY WITH ME than I thought SAFE to keep in my clothes

SO I SENT most of it HOME again,

putting a FIVE or TEN DOLLAR BILL in each letter for FATHER to KEEP for me.

But NOW the LITTLE I had kept by me was USED UP

and I had to SEND to HIM for some MORE

to pay for LAUNDRY,

STATIONARY,

and to buy SOMETHING TO EAT that I could RELISH.

At the SAME TIME I told FATHER that if he OWED any bills

he had better USE the BALANCE of it to PAY them with ....

for in MY OPINION

the TIME would SOON COME

when our GREENBACKS would be worth AS LITTLE in the NORTH

as the CONFEDERATE BILLS (which we called "RICHMOND SKINPLASTERS") were among OUR SOLDIERS.

## WARMTH

NO UNDERCLOTHES had been issued to us

except DRAWERS of thin COTTON flannel

As I have told you, we had NO STOVES

and the WEATHER, growing COLDER as the season ADVANCED,

had been RAW and DAMP ever since the RAINS set in.

JONAS was NO BETTER.

cough sniff hack cough

NEWTON was still SICK

and I was MENDING though SLOWLY

The TENT was DAMP

and the blankets as we WRAPPED them ABOUT US were CLAMMY with MOISTURE.

The ONLY CHANCE to get WARM

was to STAND in the CIRCLE of men who HUDDLED AROUND

the EMBERS of the Cook's FIRE after he was through with it.

That gave but a POOR SHOW for COMFORT.

The rest of the time we remained IN THE TENT,

either SITTING wrapped in our BLANKETS

or STRETCHED OUT on the piles of CEDAR BOUGHS we used for bunks

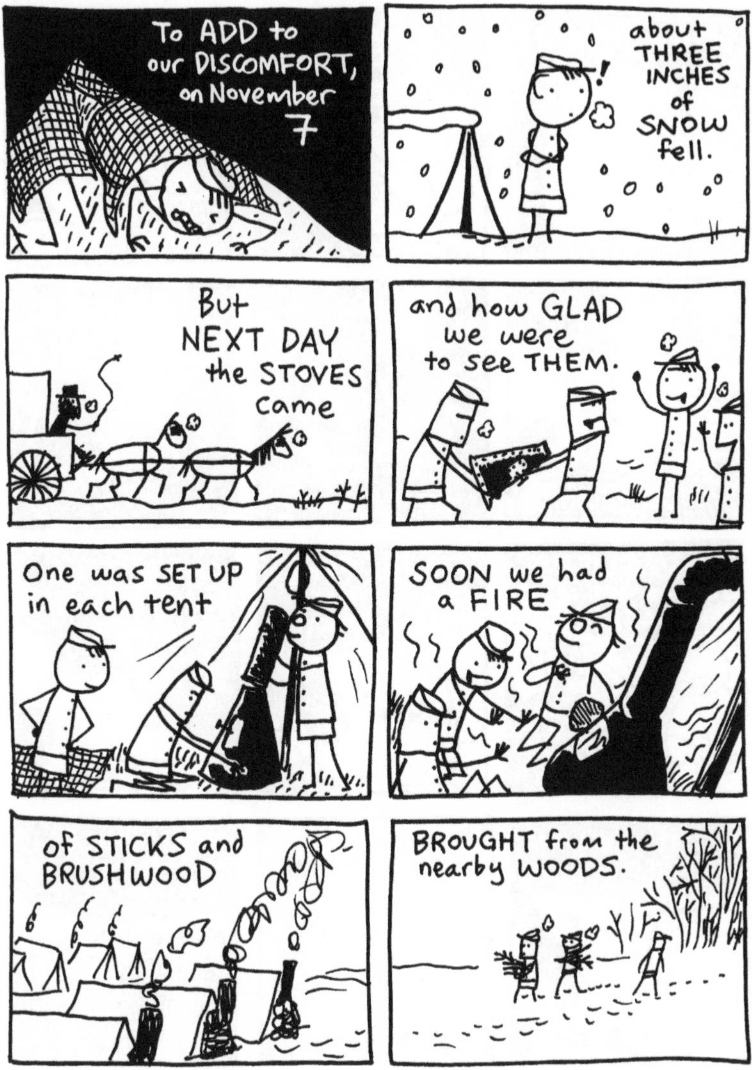
To ADD to our DISCOMFORT, on November 7
about THREE INCHES of SNOW fell.
But NEXT DAY the STOVES came
and how GLAD we were to see THEM.
One was SET UP in each tent
SOON we had a FIRE
of STICKS and BRUSHWOOD
BROUGHT from the nearby WOODS.

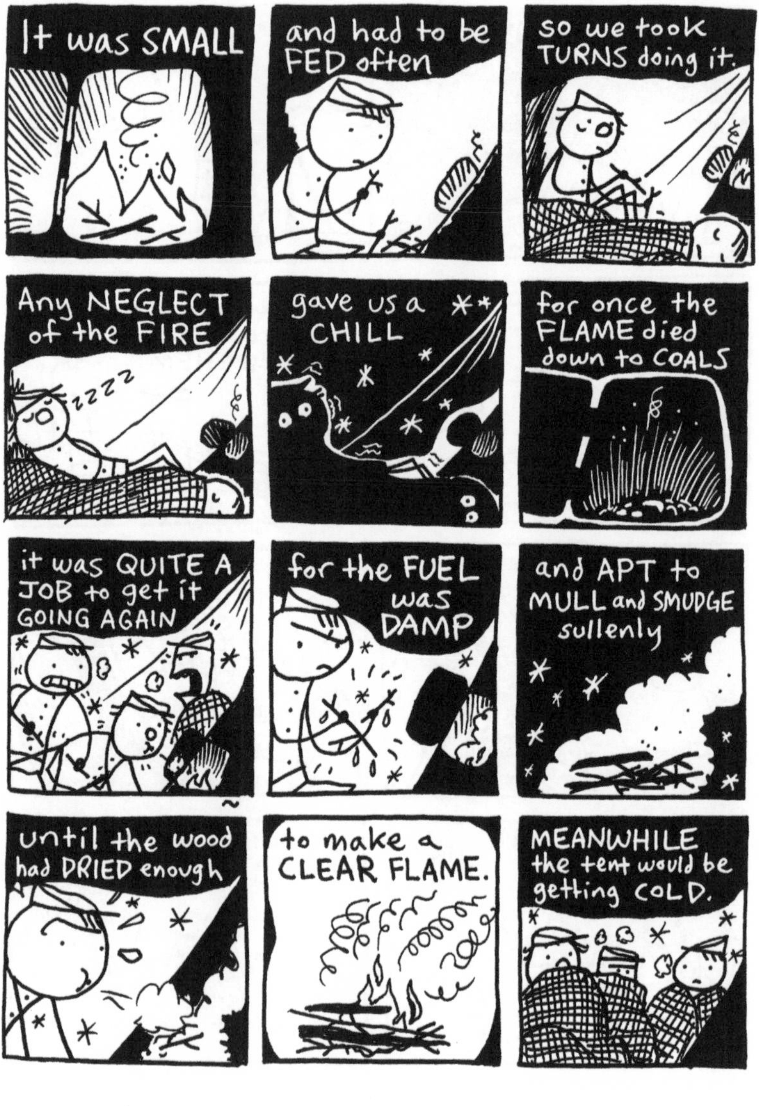
It was SMALL
and had to be FED often
so we took TURNS doing it.
Any NEGLECT of the FIRE
zzzz
gave us a CHILL
for once the FLAME died down to COALS
it was QUITE A JOB to get it GOING AGAIN
for the FUEL was DAMP
and APT to MULL and SMUDGE sullenly
until the wood had DRIED enough
to make a CLEAR FLAME.
MEANWHILE the tent would be getting COLD.

The SNOW did not STAY long but after it was GONE

the GROUND FROZE an inch or so on top

and it seemed that WINTER was indeed UPON US.

THIS made us REALIZE more than ever our PRESSING NEED of WARM UNDERWEAR,

and MITTENS

and especially an EXTRA PAIR of SHOES

So we should have a CHANGE in WET weather.

We had PUT OFF SENDING for them until NOW

as we had been EXPECTING for some time to go into WINTER QUARTERS

But NOW with the ground FROZEN under our FEET

and only our THIN CHEAP UNIFORMS for protection

it was NECESSARY to HAVE THEM as SOON as possible

So NEWTON and I WROTE HOME

to have a BOX PACKED and SENT to us at once.

We ASKED to have EVERY INCH NOT taken up by the CLOTHES

filled with PROVISIONS

for NOW was COLD and they would KEEP all right

if not TOO LONG on the ROAD.

But our STAY at MUDDY BRANCH was almost at an END.

On NOVEMBER 13 the REGIMENT LEFT the CAMP

that in one of our DREARY HOMESICK TIMES had been renamed "CAMP DESOLATION,"

for "OFFUTT'S CROSSROADS,"* five miles nearer WASHINGTON.

\* later renamed POTOMAC, MD.

# ON THE MARCH

The BUGLE SOUNDED at four o'clock.

Then followed ROLL CALL

and BREAKFAST.

Then the TENTS were taken down,

STABLES and COOK-HOUSES set on fire

(for the BOYS were BOUND

that NO ONE ELSE should ENJOY the fruits of their LABORS)

and in an HOUR and a HALF

the REGIMENT was ON THE MARCH.

The SICK were SENT to the SURGEON

who had THOSE UNABLE TO WALK carried in the WAGONS

He also TOOK CHARGE of the GUNS and KNAPSACKS of the others,

leaving them FREE to TRAVEL LIGHT.

JONAS was able to MARCH

and NEWTON was CARRIED on a team.

I thought as we had but a little over FIVE MILES to go

I would rather WALK than RIDE after a MULE TEAM

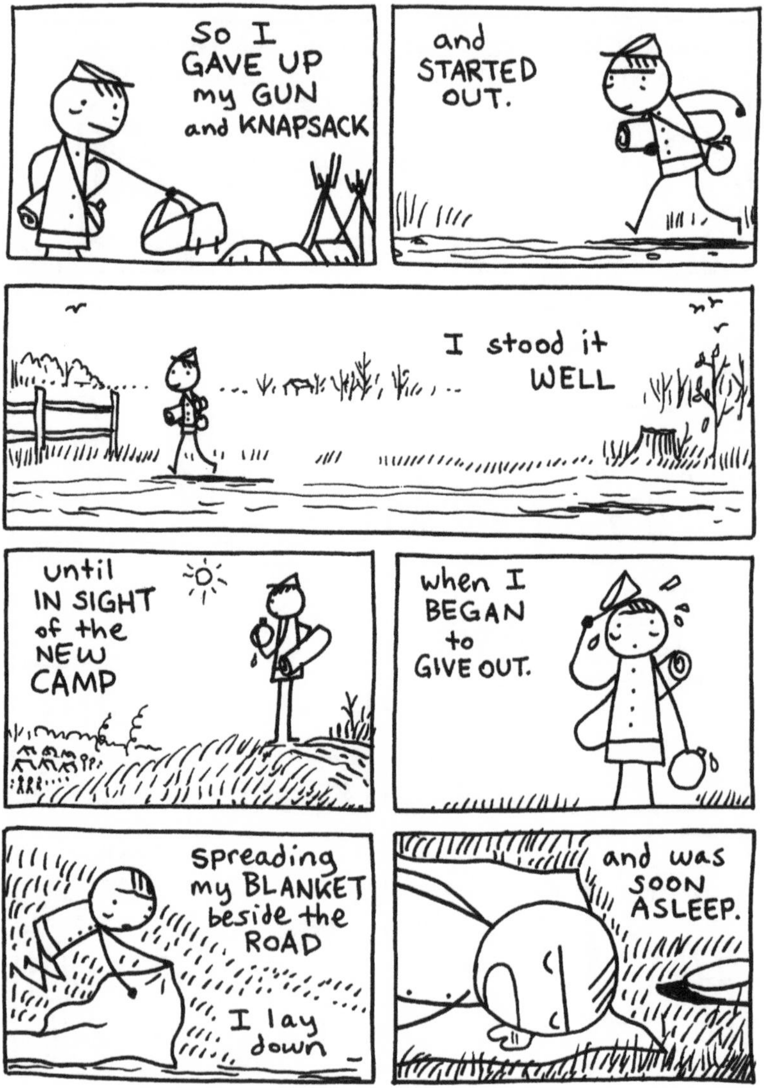
So I GAVE UP my GUN and KNAPSACK
and STARTED OUT.
I stood it WELL
until IN SIGHT of the NEW CAMP
when I BEGAN to GIVE OUT.
spreading my BLANKET beside the ROAD
I lay down
and was SOON ASLEEP.

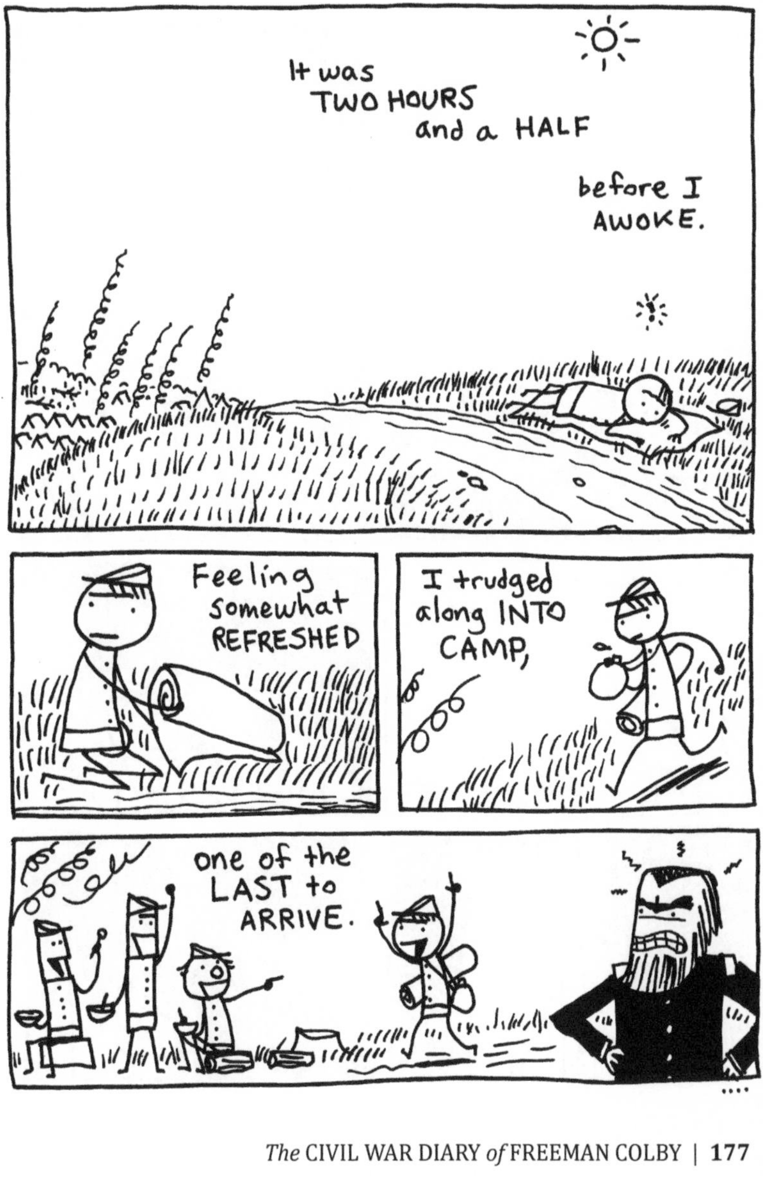
It was TWO HOURS and a HALF
before I AWOKE.
Feeling somewhat REFRESHED
I trudged along INTO CAMP,
one of the LAST to ARRIVE.
....

# RAID

We were AWAKENED that night

by a BUGLE CALL

and the ORDER was shortly PASSED to get our ARMS and EQUIPMENT READY

and be PREPARED to FALL IN at a MOMENT'S notice.

This was FOLLOWED by a RUMOR that STONEWALL JACKSON'S cavalry

were APPROACHING on one of their periodical RAIDS

But NOTHING could be learned for CERTAIN

except that we LOST a LARGE PART of our NIGHT'S SLEEP.

# OFFUTT'S CROSSROADS

The place was one of the PRETTIEST we had SEEN since GOING SOUTH.

Washington 14 miles

The FEW HOUSES were NICE and each one was GUARDED by a SENTRY.

For the FIRST WEEK of our stay there, the WEATHER was PLEASANT

with an INDIAN SUMMER WARMTH

which made the MEMORY of our recent COLD and SNOW seem like a BAD DREAM.

MANY of the LEAVES still clung to the trees,

though they were BURNED RED by the SUN and FROSTS

and RUSTLED to the ground

with every BREATH of breeze.

But this was TOO GOOD to last

and soon GAVE PLACE to a SUCCESSION of COLD, DAMP DAYS

with CLOUDY SKIES

and occasional RAIN

keeping everyone UNDER COVER

EXCEPT when ON DUTY.

About this time I got a LETTER from HOME

enclosing a FIVE DOLLAR BILL

PART of this I IMMEDIATELY INVESTED at the SUTLER'S

in the FRESH FRUIT and VEGETABLES my appetite CRAVED.

(I had got SO SHORT of MONEY that I had even SOLD my few remaining POSTAGE STAMPS to get a few PENNIES.)

~

ANY SOLDIER could SEND a LETTER without stamping it by merely marking it:

Soldier's Mail

and getting an OFFICER to SIGN his NAME to it.

This is a PRIVILEGE accorded BY LAW to United States SOLDIERS.

Such LETTERS were NOT carried for FREE,

the regular THREE CENTS POSTAGE being COLLECTED on DELIVERY.

SOMETIMES Colonel Davis signed them

but I usually got LIEUT. TREMLETT to do so for me

and a few went without being SIGNED at all.

## COMMENTS

Many of the LETTERS forwarded from the FRONT

bore on the END or BACK of the ENVELOPE

some HUMOROUS or CAUSTIC COMMENT

on the CONDUCT of the WAR

~

OR, fully as often, on the CONTINUED ABSENCE of the PAY-MASTER,

the PENNILESS CONDITION of the WRITER

and the fact that the RECEIVER was better able to PAY POSTAGE than the SENDER.

## THANKSGIVING

In our last LETTERS HOME Newton and I had both ASKED (as if that was necessary)

to be REMEMBERED at THANKSGIVING,

adding that if ANYTHING lay heavy on our STOMACHS that day

it was NOT LIKELY to be the DINNER.

# DOWN SICK

Since Newton's **SUDDEN ATTACK** while on **guard duty** at Edward's Ferry

He had been first **IN**

and then **OUT of the HOSPITAL—**

sometimes **DOWN SICK**

and then for a while **ABLE to ANSWER at ROLL CALL**

and share the **TENT** with **JONAS**, Peter Doherty, and **I**.

But he was **ALWAYS** under the **SURGEON'S CARE** and did **No heavy duty**.

He often acted as NURSE to the other SICK ONES

and was GENTLE and PATIENT with them

for WELL he KNEW how hard it was to LAY helpless on a HOSPITAL bunk

BUT as the WEATHER grew COLDER

his SUFFERINGS INCREASED

and DR. PAGE at last TOLD ME that HE could do NOTHING MORE for him

X!

while he LAY on the DAMP GROUND at night

but thought with the BETTER FOOD and NURSING to be had in WASHINGTON

that he might be BENEFITED there.

184 | MAREK BENNETT

A number of CASES needing DIFFERENT TREATMENT

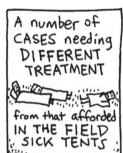

from that afforded IN THE FIELD SICK TENTS

were READY TO GO

and on NOVEMBER 20 Dr. Page SIGNED the order

for NEWTON'S TRANSFER there with them.

Besides the COMPANY, REGIMENTAL, and BRIGADE

HOSPITALS,

the Government had established GENERAL HOSPITALS at Baltimore, Philadelphia, and Washington.

To THESE were sent the CHRONIC CASES from the camps

and ALL the SURGICAL WORK was done there

EXCEPT what it was absolutely NECESSARY should be ATTENDED TO at the FRONT.

Once COMMITTED to one of THESE

a man must STAY

until he either DIED,

was CURED,

OR was given a DISCHARGE from the service.

I HEARTILY WISHED there was some way to get NEWTON a DISCHARGE at once

but NO PAPERS were given to ANYONE

X!

while there was at least a PROSPECT of their RECOVERY before their TERM of SERVICE expired

EXCEPT as a FAVOR to someone who STOOD WELL with the ADMINISTRATION.

discharge 3

It seemed to be of NO USE to even THINK of it

for WE knew NO ONE there

H.Q.

with the necessary INFLUENCE to get for him.

After the PLEASANT WEEK about the middle of NOVEMBER

when we CHANGED CAMPS,

the WEATHER turned COLD again

with RAIN nearly EVERY DAY

and as it was THOUGHT BEST NOT to SEND the SICK ONES

off to WASHINGTON

in SUCH WEATHER

they REMAINED with US

awaiting SUNSHINE and CLEAR SKIES for the TRIP down the river.

# BOXES

As THANKSGIVING drew near

the BOYS commenced to TALK

of the GOOD THINGS they expected to GET when their BOXES came.

Many besides OURSELVES had SENT HOME for EXTRA CLOTHES

and with the HOLIDAY in mind

EACH ONE had his mind on the GENEROUS SHARE of PROVISIONS the family would be SURE to PUT IN.

but NOT A BOX arrived until the 28th,

which, for a WONDER, was WARM and PLEASANT

when the GOOD NEWS spread around that they had COME.

They were TAKEN AT ONCE to HEADQUARTERS

but BEFORE being DELIVERED to their OWNERS

EACH BOX was OPENED by the officers.

For THIS, a FEE of FIVE CENTS was charged

and to PROMOTE the cause of TEMPERANCE among the PRIVATES

they TOOK OUT all the LIQUOR they found

....

and SAVED IT for THEMSELVES.

And a FINE DRUNK they had that NIGHT with it, too. They ALL got together

and the QUARTERMASTER FIDDLED for them

while THEY emptied the BOTTLES.

HE did his part at THAT, too.

When the LIQUOR was nearly GONE

COLONEL DAVIS and GENERAL GROVER (who had just got back from WASHINGTON)

Spent about an HOUR trying to GET HIM to SING a SONG.

One of the CAPTAINS LOST his COAT

and more than HALF the crowd were UNFIT FOR DUTY next day.

But the OBJECT of their CARE for OUR GOOD was accomplished

for EVERY PRIVATE remained perfectly SOBER —

though the CURSES of some of them were DEEP and ELOQUENT

and they WISHED the OFFICERS MAROONED on the SEWARD ISLANDS

where LIQUOR is still HARDER to get than it is in the ARMY.

# KNIFE

The men in COMPANY K alone received about FIFTY BOXES

I KNEW they were to be SEARCHED

So I TOOK CARE to be around

HEADQUARTERS

when MINE was OPENED.

ONE of the things it CONTAINED

was a FINE POCKET KNIFE father had BOUGHT for me.

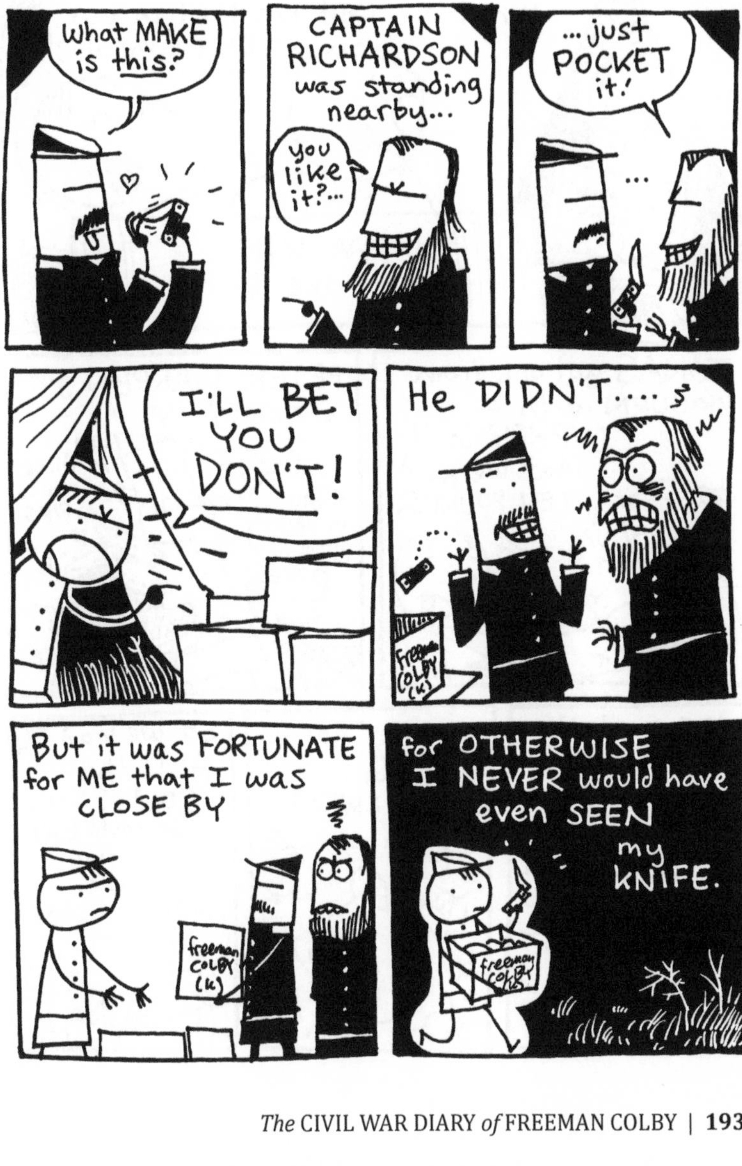
What MAKE is this?
CAPTAIN RICHARDSON was standing nearby...
you like it?...
...just POCKET it!
...
I'LL BET YOU DON'T!
He DIDN'T....
FREEMAN COLBY (K)
But it was FORTUNATE for ME that I was CLOSE BY
freeman COLBY (K)
for OTHERWISE I NEVER would have even SEEN my KNIFE.
freeman COLBY

# UNPACKING

What a TIME we had in our TENT that night

UNPACKING the boxes.

JONAS got one from WOBURN with a TURKEY in it that weighed TEN POUNDS.

PETER WARREN got a TURKEY ♡

a BIG PLUM PUDDING

♡ three mince PIES

and LOTS of CAKE

ALSO a bottle of JAUNDICE BITTERS (which the officers had NOT confiscated).

TOMMY got a BIG CHICKEN

so we had ALL the COLD FOWL we could EAT for SOME DAYS.

194 | MAREK BENNETT

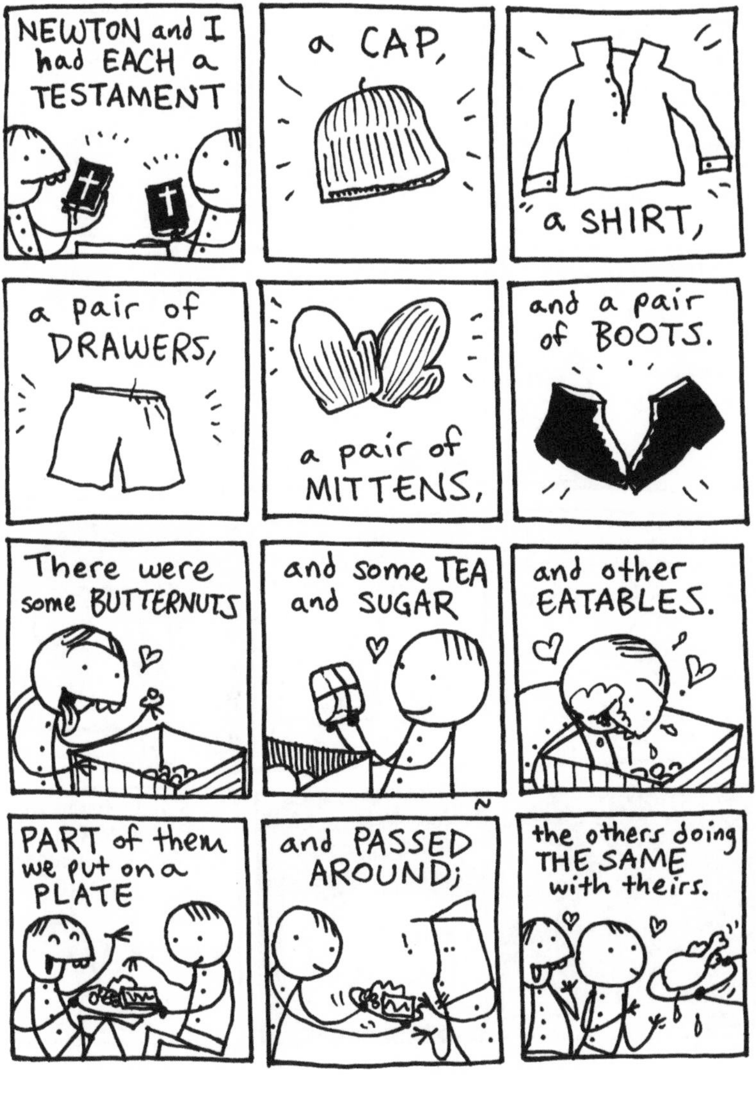
NEWTON and I had EACH a TESTAMENT
a CAP,
a SHIRT,
a pair of DRAWERS,
a pair of MITTENS,
and a pair of BOOTS.
There were some BUTTERNUTS
and some TEA and SUGAR
and other EATABLES.
PART of them we put on a PLATE
and PASSED AROUND;
the others doing THE SAME with theirs.

We were DISAPPOINTED at finding NO STAMPS or STATIONARY

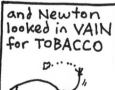
and Newton looked in VAIN for TOBACCO

as he had COUNTED on getting a FRESH SUPPLY

But every single thing was JUST what we WANTED

EXCEPT my BOOTS which were VERY LIGHT

and NOT MUCH BETTER in the MUD than the ARMY SHOES.

LATER ON they gave me a great deal of COMFORT

for when we got into WINTER QUARTERS

I could SIT on the EDGE of my BUNK

and KICK them OFF

without even TOUCHING THEM with my HANDS.

I SOLD them in FEBRUARY for $2.50 and bought some a little NEARER my size.

# TEA

When we had EATEN our FILL of the provisions ~burp!~

I BOILED some water on the TENT STOVE

and BREWED a dipper of TEA for each of us

before we TURNED IN.

For a SHORT TIME when we FIRST went OUT THERE TEA had been served ONCE IN A WHILE as part of the RATION

but it was NOT the kind that MOTHER used to make

and SOON DISAPPEARED entirely

for COFFEE was CHEAPER and LIKED by everyone.

# SAGE

 The NEXT night I made SAGE TEA.

 How many MEMORIES were recalled by its FRAGRANCE —

 of WINTER EVENINGS by the HOME FIRESIDE

 when MOTHER used to give us EACH a steaming BOWL of it to WARD OFF a possible COLD.

 Grown in the "Lower Garden" where the SWEET FLAGS stood in the old TAN PITS

 and PICKED by MOTHER and the GIRLS it's FLAVOR seemed to BRING them a little bit NEARER—

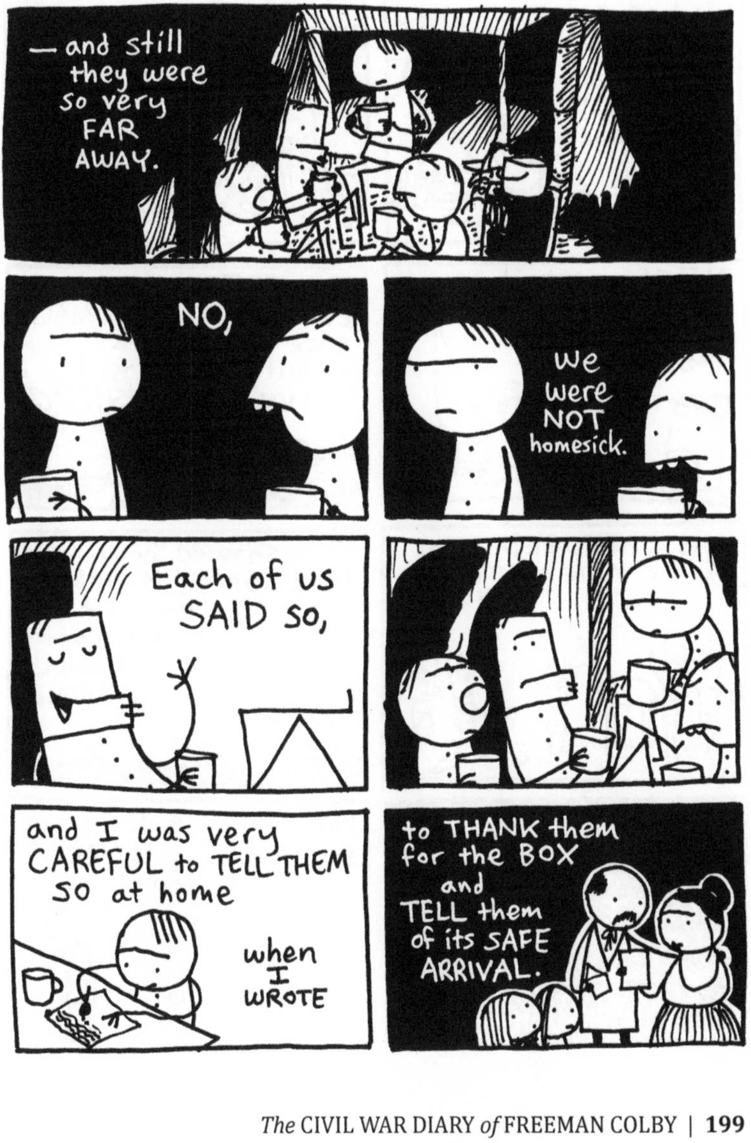
— and still they were so very FAR AWAY.
NO,
we were NOT homesick.
Each of us SAID so,
and I was very CAREFUL to TELL THEM so at home
when I WROTE
to THANK them for the BOX and TELL them of its SAFE ARRIVAL.

# ANOTHER REBEL RAID

We had got our TENTS fairly well FIXED UP for winter,

as we thought it BEST if another COLD SPELL came on to be PREPARED,

BUT it was said we were SOON to MOVE again.

The REBELS had CROSSED the POTOMAC once more in the vicinity of POOLVILLE

and CAPTURED some of our MEN and TEAMS there.

This showed how NECESSARY it was that the RIVER remain STRONGLY GUARDED

and WE might expect to take another turn SOON at PICKET DUTY.

For MY part, I did not see HOW I could MARCH any distance for I was still FAR from STRONG.

# RECOVERY

The SURGEON would NEVER tell a patient much about his CASE.

He ASKED QUESTIONS,

DEALT OUT medicine,

and looked WISE.

But I learned from LIEUTENANT WYMAN

that he thought I had taken MEDICINE enough

and what I NEEDED NOW was REST

and a LIGHT DIET while my STRENGTH RETURNED.

This it seemed in NO HURRY to do.

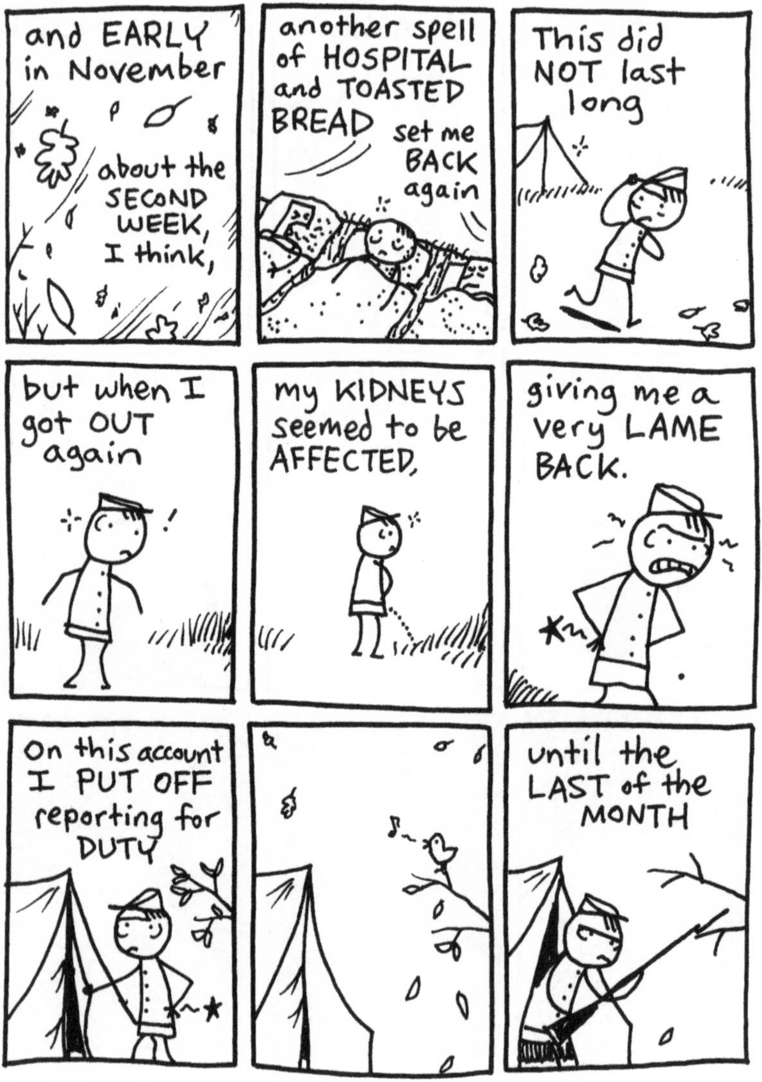
and EARLY in November
about the SECOND WEEK, I think,
another spell of HOSPITAL and TOASTED BREAD
set me BACK again
This did NOT last long
but when I got OUT again
my KIDNEYS seemed to be AFFECTED,
giving me a very LAME BACK.
On this account I PUT OFF reporting for DUTY
until the LAST of the MONTH

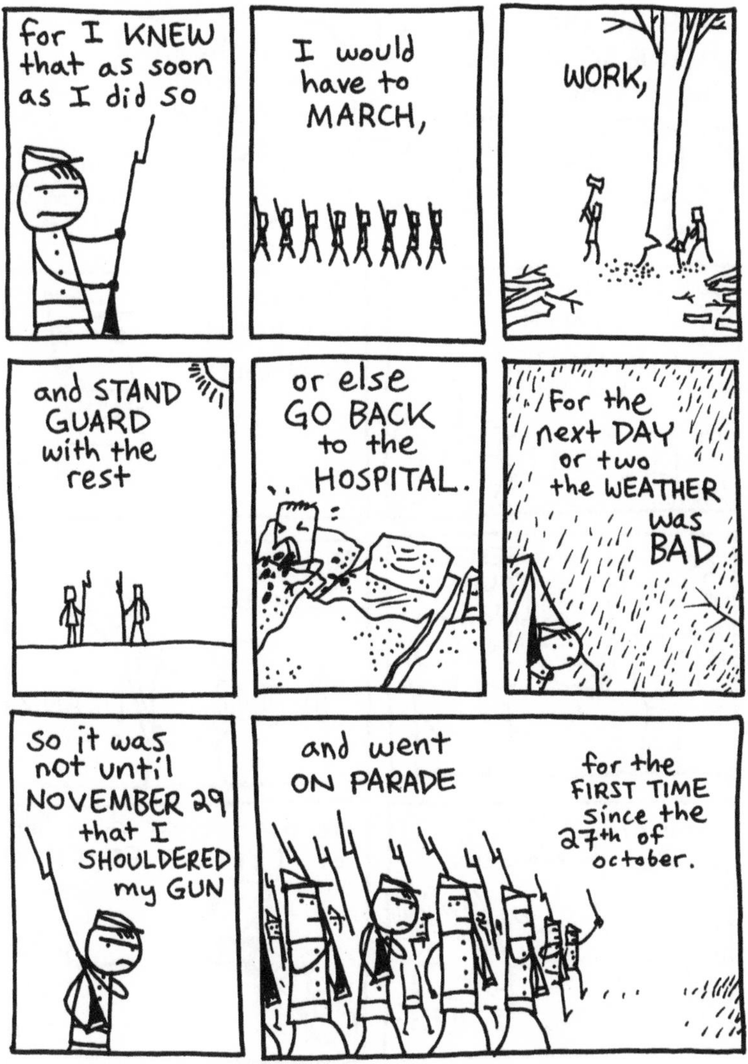
for I KNEW that as soon as I did so
I would have to MARCH,
WORK,
and STAND GUARD with the rest
or else GO BACK to the HOSPITAL.
For the next DAY or two the WEATHER was BAD
so it was not until NOVEMBER 29 that I SHOULDERED my GUN
and went ON PARADE
for the FIRST TIME since the 27th of october.

With all the SICKNESS in the Regiment

there had been BUT ONE DEATH

after the man was POISONED in BALTIMORE

until NOVEMBER 17th,

but BEFORE the END of the MONTH SIX MORE had DIED.

The LAST was HUGH CONNOLLY,

who SEEMED as TOUGH as ANY man in the army.

But he was RECKLESS,

DRANK a good deal

and didn't TAKE CARE of himself.

He died that day of TYPHOID FEVER.

OF OUR COMPANY alone there were FOUR MEN in the HOSPITAL

and TWENTY-THREE MORE on the SICK LIST but remained in their own QUARTERS.

ONE of those in the HOSPITAL was NOT expected to LIVE.

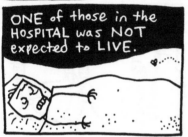

OTHER REGIMENTS were MUCH WORSE OFF than ours.

The 10TH VERMONT, which arrived at WASHINGTON the same night WE did

had LOST over FORTY men.

SUCH a MORTALITY RECORD would NOW be thought to imply CRIMINAL NEGLIGENCE on SOMEONE'S part

but NO NOTICE was taken of it THEN

nor any CRITICISM made of the SURGEONS,

OFFICERS,

or the ADMINISTRATION at Washington

except by the

PEACE AT ANY PRICE!

NEWSPAPERS of the North

and THESE only used it as an ARGUMENT for:

COMPROMISE with the REBELS!

# SUNDAY

The last day of NOVEMBER

dawned clear and MILD

and such a STILL, QUIET day—

the STILLEST I had EVER seen in the army.

Brigade Inspection,

dress parade,

and five FUNERALS.

The rest of the TIME we had to ourselves.

There were no DEVOTIONAL SERVICES of any sort.

Indeed, there had been but THREE held in camp since we left HOME

and only ONE of these was held by our CHAPLAIN.

FEW of us more than KNEW him by sight

for he did the WILL of GOD

by CARRYING ON a LIGHT EXPRESS BUSINESS between the CAMP and WASHINGTON.

This, and SELLING STATIONARY to the MEN,

kept HIM very BUSY seven days in the WEEK.

# TRANSFER

THAT AFTERNOON it was announced that the SICK ONES who had been ordered TRANSFERRED to Washington

were to GO BY BOAT early the next morning.

The LONG WAIT for GOOD WEATHER had WORN on Newton's NERVES

but no one could BLAME HIM in the least for being IRRITABLE

as the SUCCESSION of RAW DRIZZLY days

was ENOUGH to DEPRESS the SPIRITS of the MOST cheerful,

while to be SICK and SHUT UP in our COMFORTLESS QUARTERS

with others but LITTLE BETTER OFF than himself

would have SPOILED the TEMPER of a JOB.

NOW that he was about to LEAVE

I almost ENVIED him

and yet at the same time I was SORRY to see him GO.

NEXT MORNING, December 1,

I went with him to the BOAT.

There were about FIFTY SICK MEN being sent off

& as the distance to WASHINGTON by CANAL was only about 14 miles, they would BE THERE by night.

This was WELL, as there was NO SHELTER for the men

should a STORM COME UP while they were ON THE WAY.

BEFORE we STARTED, I had BOUGHT for him

a dozen sheets of PAPER, as many ENVELOPES,

and a LOAF of SOFT BREAD.

And now I SHARED with him the little MONEY I had left.

$2.60

He PROMISED to WRITE to me

and ALSO to the FOLKS at HOME as soon as he COULD.

We had but LITTLE TIME to talk

as the BOAT was soon LOADED,

the LITTERS or COTS in two LINES

leaving an ALLEY between

and the ENDS FREE for the CREW to WORK.

When all was READY

We said a HURRIED GOODBYE

and I stepped ASHORE

JUST as the word to START was given

*The* CIVIL WAR DIARY *of* FREEMAN COLBY | **211**

and the BOAT commenced to MOVE.

# HOPE

I tried to CONSOLE MYSELF as I went back to CAMP

by thinking that his TRANSFER was for the BEST

and that he would SOON be CURED

OR sent HOME,

But even with this HOPE in mind

. . . .

it was but a SORRY PARTING

and the CONVERSATION of the men around me was NOT of a sort to LIGHTEN my MISGIVINGS.

*The* CIVIL WAR DIARY *of* FREEMAN COLBY | **213**

My TENTMATES made an EFFORT to speak HOPEFULLY of his PROSPECTS

but our EXPERIENCE with the Regimental SURGEONS had NOT been such as to INSPIRE US

with OVERMUCH CONFIDENCE in their SKILL

or RESPECT for their DEVOTION to our WELFARE.

OF COURSE, it was UNFAIR to JUDGE the WASHINGTON DOCTORS by them,

but I could NOT HELP THINKING

that he might be KEPT THERE

and EXPERIMENTED on by some young SAWBONES

and if he DIED there

perhaps neither I NOR the folks at HOME

would KNOW about it until LONG AFTERWARDS.

We MISSED him greatly

and the TENT seemed very EMPTY after he was GONE.

EVERY DAY some of the boys would INQUIRE for NEWS of him

but tho I EXPECTED a LETTER from him SOON

NONE CAME...

...until the **ELEVENTH**.

With it was a **NEWSPAPER**.

He had **MAILED** them **BOTH** from **ST. ALOISIN'S HOSPITAL** the day after he got there

and they had been **TEN DAYS** on the way —

**FOURTEEN MILES** in **TEN days** —

and **I ANXIOUSLY WAITING** to hear from him.

He only wrote to say he had **STOOD** the **TRIP** well

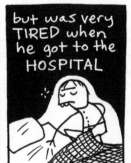

but was very **TIRED** when he got to the **HOSPITAL**

and would **WRITE AGAIN SOON** to tell me how he was **GETTING ON**.

ADVOCATE

The NEXT DAY while I was WRITING a LETTER HOME

One of the boys CAME IN with the NEWS:

PARKER RICHARDSON is in camp!

He was one of our REPRESENTATIVES in CONGRESS,

and had just COME FROM WASHINGTON

where he had seen MANY of our SICK ONES

and was NOW on his way to visit his SON at HILTON HEAD.*

#OCCUPIED South Carolina.

As he was WELL THOUGHT OF at Woburn and had some INFLUENCE at Washington,

I at once went to LOOK HIM UP

with a view to getting him INTERESTED in NEWTON'S WELFARE.

Sniff

| | | |
|---|---|---|
| I found him TALKING with a group of the boys  | and soon learned that he was planning to TAKE a PARTY of HOME-BOUND men  | BACK WITH HIM to Massachusetts.  |
| He readily PROMISED to LOOK NEWTON UP  | and if he were NOT ALREADY discharged,  | to get his PAPERS for him  |
| and take him BACK along with the rest.  | This did a LOT to CHEER me up  | and was ALL I could ASK of him,  |
| but it left me as much IN THE DARK as ever  | as to what HAPPENED to NEWTON since the DAY AFTER he got to the HOSPITAL. | Indeed, it was SEVERAL WEEKS before I heard so much as a WORD from him.  |

For a while after Newton left us the WEATHER was PLEASANT and WARM,

more like SEPTEMBER & OCTOBER in NEW ENGLAND than the sort of WEATHER WE were accustomed to in DECEMBER.

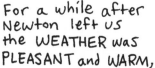

We KNEW this COULD NOT last long

SO I WROTE HOME for another BOX

thinking that BY THE TIME they got around to SEND it

the WEATHER would surely be COLD enough

so FOOD would KEEP on the way.

# HERE IS A LIST OF WHAT I ASKED FOR: ~

 Some
SLIPPERY
ELM bark,

 a little
GINGER,

 some
SWEET FLAG
root,

 a bunch of
DRIED APPLES,

 a few
NUTMEGS
and a
GRATER,

 some
CHESNUTS
and some
BONESET
or a few stick
of COUGH CANDY.

I wanted
some BUTTER

but as
JONAS
did not
eat
butter,

I asked mother
to put in a piece
of HOMEMADE
CHEESE for him.

IF they had made their
SAUSAGES in STRINGS
that year,

then I wanted a few
FRIED and PUT IN

for I had tasted
NOTHING so GOOD
since leaving HOME

as a
SAUSAGE
and BOILED
EGG someone
gave me.

~

Then a small BAKED SPARERIB

and LAST but by no means LEAST

half a pound of CHEWING TOBACCO

 for I had taken to CHEWING since coming out

as I didn't seem to RELISH my PIPE as much as formerly.

This was ALL I could think of when I WROTE

but, of course,

as soon as the LETTER was MAILED

I RECALLED several more things I had MEANT to send for.

*The* CIVIL WAR DIARY *of* FREEMAN COLBY | **221**

# PARTY

One night near Christmas time

CAPTAIN NELSON (of the next company)

(whose TENT was right back of OURS)

got in a CROWD of fellows, mostly officers,

for a GOOD TIME.

This meant CARDS and plenty of WHISKEY

which, though CONTRABAND, could usually be HAD by PAYING ENOUGH for it.

The ARMY REGULATIONS said

that OFFICERS MUST NOT DRINK while ON DUTY

but didn't mention getting DRUNK ENOUGH at night.

We didn't doubt they had a RIGHT to

but when they got NOISY along towards MIDNIGHT

and kept us AWAKE,

We had OBJECTIONS

and were NOT AT ALL BASHFUL about letting them be KNOWN.

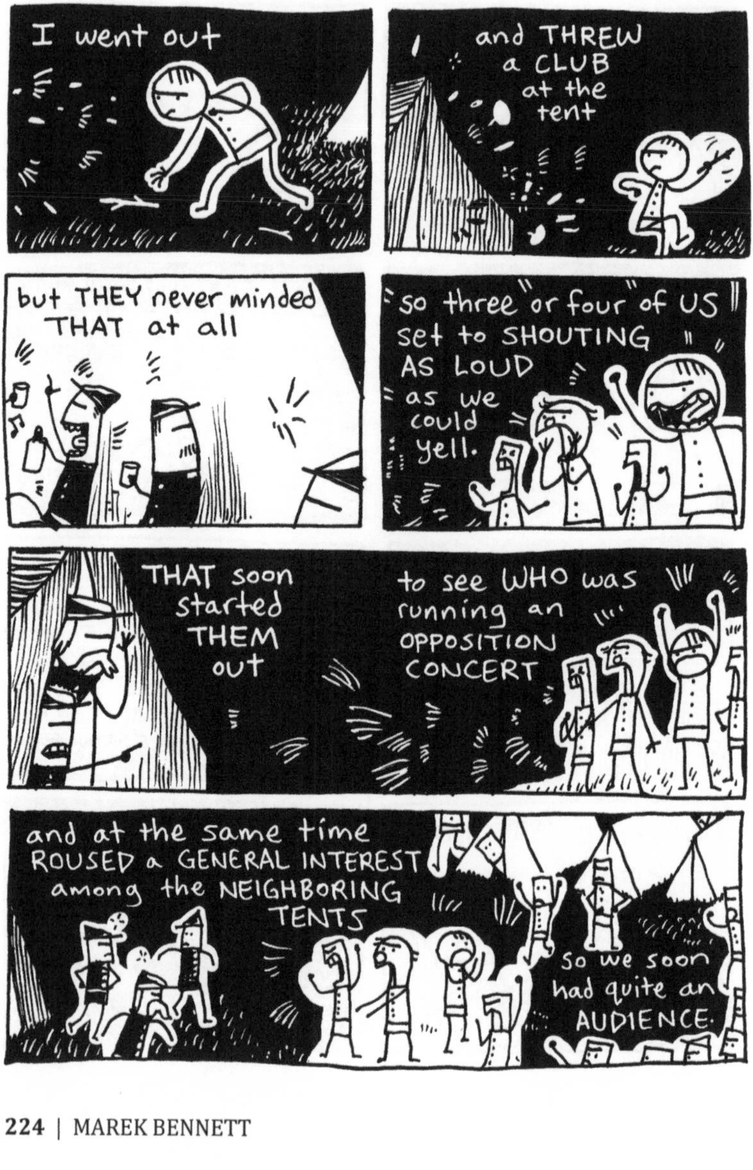
I went out
and THREW a CLUB at the tent
but THEY never minded THAT at all
so three or four of US set to SHOUTING AS LOUD as we could yell.
THAT soon started THEM out
to see WHO was running an OPPOSITION CONCERT
and at the same time ROUSED a GENERAL INTEREST among the NEIGHBORING TENTS
so we soon had quite an AUDIENCE.

Just then LIEUTENANT TIDD came along...

Be still!

I'll REPORT Captain Nelson in the morning.

While we were talking,

the CAPTAIN came up behind us

and HEARD what was SAID

So when the LIEUTENANT turned to go,

they met FACE to FACE.

They immediately COMMENCED to JAW

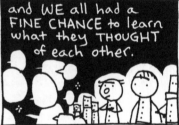

and WE all had a FINE CHANCE to learn what they THOUGHT of each other.

There were plenty of COMMENTS by the MEN standing about

and tho they DIDN'T come to BLOWS, it was pretty WARM

and when the CAPTAIN went back to his TENT

he was left in NO DOUBT as to what WE thought of him...

You're a MISERABLE DRUNKEN CUS

and NOT FIT to be an OFFICER in the REAR RANK!

This was FREE ENOUGH COMMENTS to be sure

flap!

but HE was NO OFFICER of OURS

and WE ALL felt it to be JUSTIFIED.

The FRIDAY before Christmas

I was on the DETAIL to SUPPLY the Company FUEL.

After CHOPPING and CARRYING my share of the WOOD

I found myself WELL TIRED OUT at night

and WOKE next morning with BACK and KIDNEYS as SORE as ever.

At SICK CALL I reported to the SURGEON

who, after asking me a few QUESTIONS, MARKED me for QUARTERS.

This was LUCKY for me but I DIDN'T KNOW IT until later.

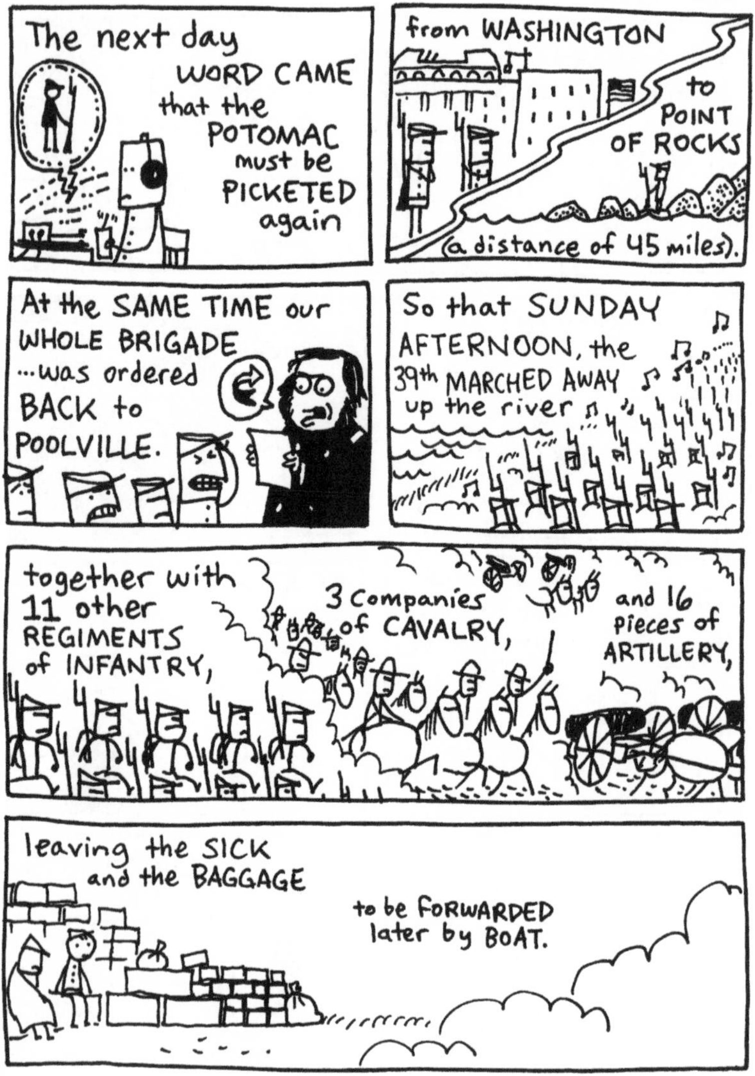
The next day
WORD CAME that the POTOMAC must be PICKETED again
from WASHINGTON
to POINT OF ROCKS
(a distance of 45 miles).
At the SAME TIME our WHOLE BRIGADE ...was ordered BACK to POOLVILLE.
So that SUNDAY AFTERNOON, the 39th MARCHED AWAY up the river
together with 11 other REGIMENTS of INFANTRY,
3 Companies of CAVALRY,
and 16 pieces of ARTILLERY,
leaving the SICK and the BAGGAGE
to be FORWARDED later by BOAT.

# HARDTACK & COFFEE

...The next MORNING I LEFT the camp

which was now being ABANDONED

and went down to an old STORE HOUSE near the canal...

to WAIT while the BOAT was being LOADED.

It took ALL the REST of the DAY to do it

and at last I grew HUNGRY.

There was a BAKERY nearby

FRESH BREAD = 5¢

but I had USED the LAST CENT of money

AND SOLD my POSTAGE STAMPS

to buy SUGAR for my TEA

So NOW I had to be CONTENT

AS USUAL with HARDTACK and COFFEE.

# ICE

Towards NIGHT

when the TENTS and other LUGGAGE had all been STOWED AWAY

the SICK were CARRIED on board

and made as COMFORTABLE as possible.

Then we SET SAIL up the CANAL

behind a MULE TEAM.

They TOWED us as far as SENECA MILLS that night

but THERE we had to STOP

on account of the ICE.

My bed for the NIGHT was a PILE of BOXES.

I had a SINGLE BLANKET over me

but SOME of the men had NONE at all.

230 | MAREK BENNETT

AFTER the ICE was ploughed out

* we started AGAIN

and late in the FORENOON reached the END of our canal boat trip

but we were still FIVE MILES from Poolesville.

Those of us who were ABLE,

MARCHED there,

carrying NO LOAD,

and were QUARTERED in a CHURCH.

## SURROUNDED

THIS CHURH was where 25 of our CAVALRYMEN had been CAPTURED while attending a PRAYER MEETING some time before.

They had been LEFT THERE

when the REST of the troops were ORDERED AWAY

and were SUPPOSED to be doing GUARD DUTY

for EVERYONE KNEW that MOST of the COUNTY were REBELS

tho MANY of them professed STRONG UNION SENTIMENTS

whenever ANY of our TROOPS were NEAR.
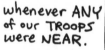

MANY of them had been DRAFTED into the UNION ARMY

but being SECESSIONISTS at heart

they would take the FIRST OPPORTUNITY to RUN AWAY

and CROSS OVER to their REBEL FRIENDS in Virginia.

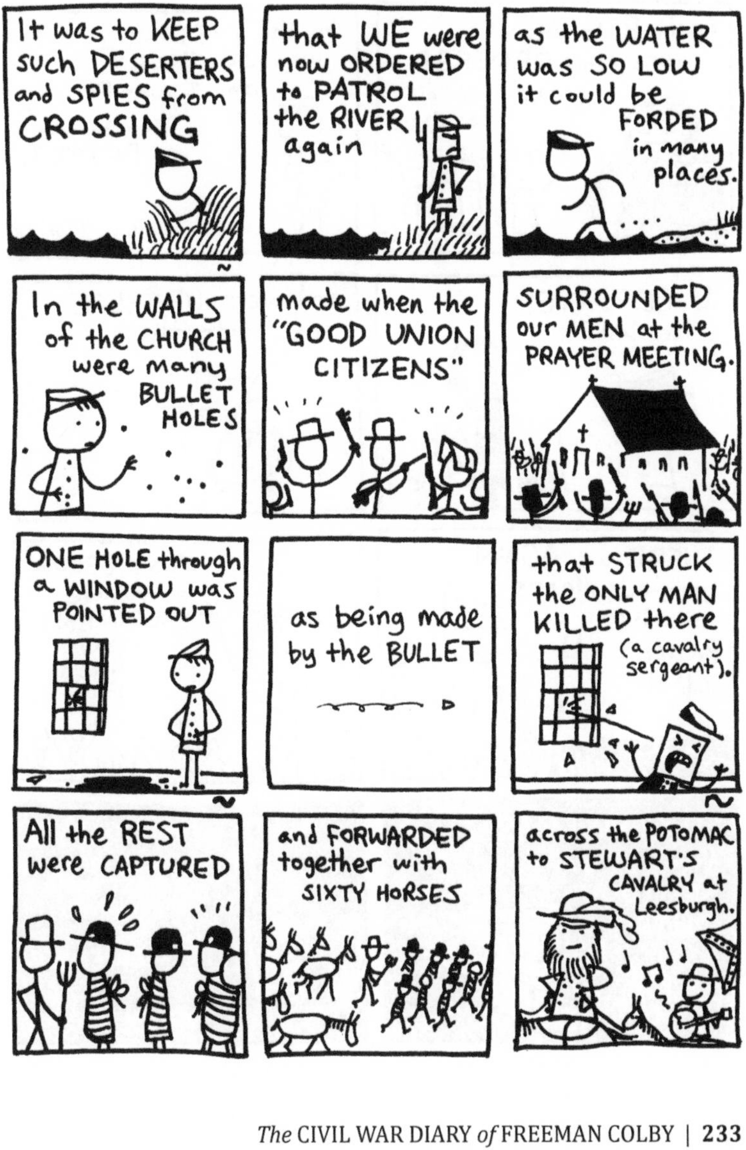
It was to KEEP such DESERTERS and SPIES from CROSSING
that WE were now ORDERED to PATROL the RIVER again
as the WATER was SO LOW it could be FORDED in many places.
In the WALLS of the CHURCH were many BULLET HOLES
made when the "GOOD UNION CITIZENS"
SURROUNDED our MEN at the PRAYER MEETING.
ONE HOLE through a WINDOW was POINTED OUT
as being made by the BULLET
that STRUCK the ONLY MAN KILLED there
(a cavalry sergeant).
All the REST were CAPTURED
and FORWARDED together with SIXTY HORSES
across the POTOMAC to STEWART'S CAVALRY at Leesburgh.

OUR REGIMENT was now ORDERED to Edward's Ferry.

As the DISTANCE was SO SHORT and I was feeling somewhat BETTER,

I REPORTED for DUTY

and went UP THERE with them.

THERE, we AGAIN took our places on the PICKET LINE

JUST BELOW a MAINE REGIMENT near White's Ford.

SO CHRISTMAS found us doing SENTRY DUTY

in ALMOST the very place we had FIRST COME TO early in SEPTEMBER.

Here I got a LETTER from home

enclosing some MORE MONEY

and FULL of anxious INQUIRIES as to my HEALTH and SPIRITS

and wanting to KNOW if the STORIES printed in NORTHERN PAPERS

of pickets SHOT

or FROZEN at their posts

and the BARBAROUS TREATMENT of PRISONERS by the rebels

were TRUE?

I REPLIED at once that I was SORRY to have them WORRY about ME,

ASSURING them that I was NEARLY WELL again and doing my REGULAR DUTY,

and had NEVER been in BETTER SPIRITS

or ENJOYED myself MORE than since I had GOT ABOUT again.

I had not HEARD of anyone being FROZEN

and did not BELIEVE it could be TRUE

for our COLDEST WEATHER SO far would HARDLY freeze a MAN'S EARS

and we ALL had PLENTY of CLOTHING to keep us WARM.

## COMFORT

For myself, I had EVERYTHING I needed for COMFORT EXCEPT some TOWELS.

MINE had been STOLEN a day or two before.

I could play the SAME GAME if necessary

but I rather preferred to BUY some now I had a little MONEY once more.

## STANDING ORDERS

I told them that the NORTHERN and SOUTHERN GENERALS had made an AGREEMENT

the previous June

to PROHIBIT the SHOOTING of PICKETS by either side.

We had STANDING ORDERS NOT to SHOOT at the REBEL PICKETS

under penalty of COURTS MARTIAL.

*The* CIVIL WAR DIARY *of* FREEMAN COLBY | **237**

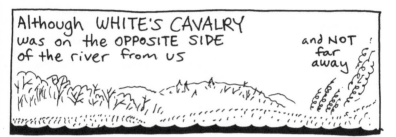

Although WHITE'S CAVALRY was on the OPPOSITE SIDE of the river from us and NOT far away

we NEVER heard a GUN FIRED

except at some unlucky cow, PIG, goose, or DUCK.

There were LOTS of DUCKS in the river

and we saw FLOCK after FLOCK on the WING,

which must have numbered at least TWO HUNDRED.

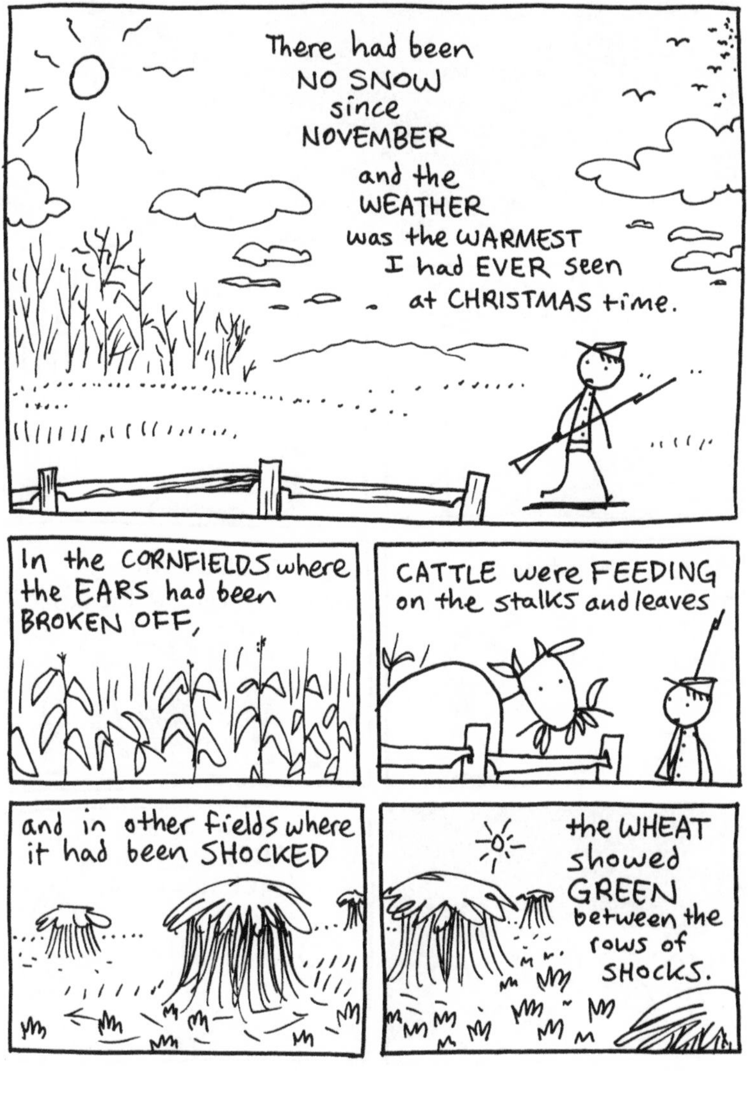
There had been NO SNOW since NOVEMBER
and the WEATHER was the WARMEST I had EVER seen at CHRISTMAS time.
In the CORNFIELDS where the EARS had been BROKEN OFF,
CATTLE were FEEDING on the stalks and leaves
and in other fields where it had been SHOCKED
the WHEAT showed GREEN between the rows of SHOCKS.

# HOLIDAYS AT THE SOUTH

Before Christmas we saw the NEGROES HUSKING by a BIG FIRE after a day's WORK at PLOUGHING

and NEXT MORNING there would be GREAT HEAPS of CORN

to cart to the RAIL PENS to be stored.

After Christmas they did LITTLE work for FIFTEEN DAYS or so

for THEIR holidays only COMMENCED the 25th...

During that time they seemed to GO nearly where they LIKED

and certainly ate ALL the CHICKENS they could get HOLD OF.

# CHRISTMAS

Our CHRISTMAS was just like any other day.

No PRESENTS,

no Christmas DINNER,

only the REGULAR ROUNDS of duty—

but our MINDS were often BUSY with thoughts of HOME

and memories of OTHER Christmas days

After only TWO DAYS of Edward's Ferry we were ordered back to Poolesville.

The MAINE REGIMENT that was to take our PLACES came up on a BOAT the morning after CHRISTMAS

and that AFTERNOON we MARCHED back to the LANDING,

filed ON BOARD

and were towed to POOLSVILLE

where we understood we were to go into WINTER QUARTERS.

.... This was the HEADQUARTERS of SIEGEL'S CORPS

and as OURS was the FIRST BRIGADE we were assigned to the PLACE OF HONOR at the RIGHT of the CAMP...

# NEGLECT

It seemed our OFFICERS expected us to be ordered to MOVE AGAIN SOON

for VERY FEW MEN were allowed to go home on FURLOUGHS

X!

and they NEGLECTED to PROVIDE many of the COMFORTS and CONVENIENCES we might have had with a little WORK...

For one thing, our WATER SUPPLY was drawn from some DISTANCE.

This was a VERY UNHANDY arrangement,

but it was MONTHS before WELLS were dug to give us PLENTY of GOOD WATER close at hand.

# DUTY

When we ARRIVED there the POTOMAC was still very LOW

So to PROTECT ourselves from a quick CROSSING of it by the JOHNNIES

and a SURPRISE,

it was thought NECESSARY to PICKET all the ROADS about the CAMP

and to keep a GUARD in the village.

In addition to this, we were REQUIRED for a while

to keep our GUNS LOADED

and SLEEP with our EQUIPMENT ALL ON

READY at a BUGLE CALL

~

to FALL in LINE,

READY to REPEL an ATTACK.

# PLENTY TO DO

EVIDENTLY we were not to be ALLOWED to feel TOO SECURE and so get RUSTY

For EVERY AFTERNOON we DRILLED for 2½ HOURS.

But the number of DAILY CALLS was cut down from TEN

to FOUR.

There was PLENTY TO DO at that

for our regiment had to keep 36 MEN on PICKET,

50 on PROVOST GUARD, &

10 on CAMP GUARD

and 21 ON GUARD at the General's HEADQUARTERS

BESIDES a daily detail of 30 MEN

to CHOP the WOOD needed for building BLOCK HOUSES

and for FUEL.

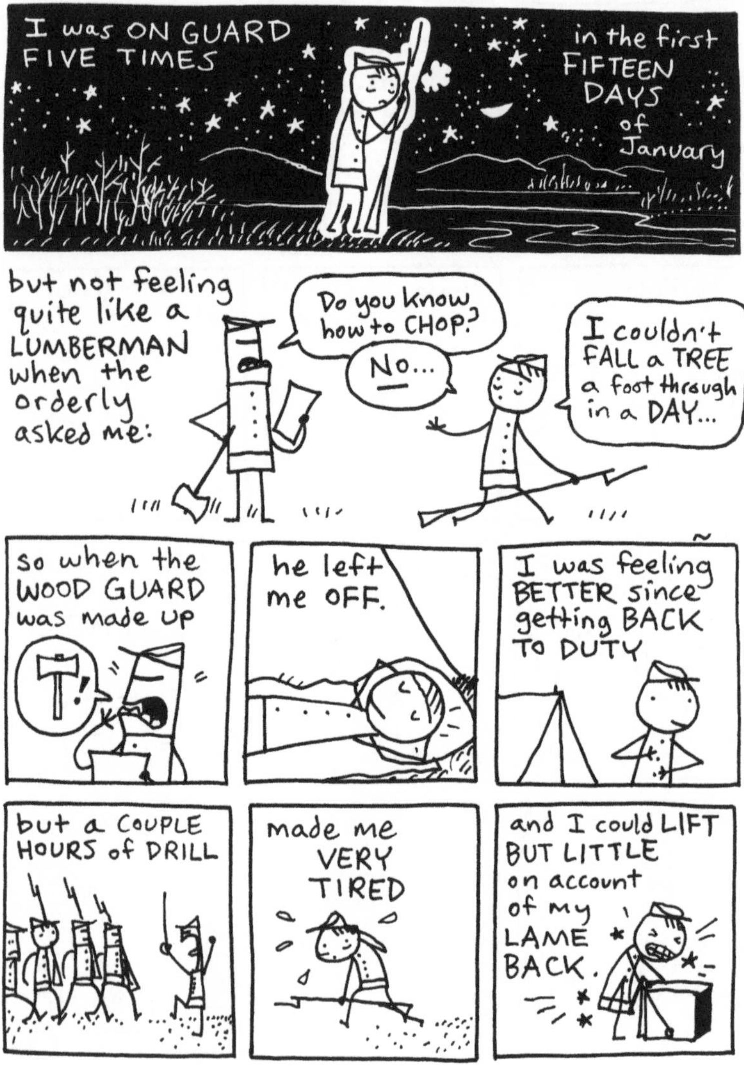
I was ON GUARD FIVE TIMES
in the first FIFTEEN DAYS of January
but not feeling quite like a LUMBERMAN when the orderly asked me:
Do you know how to CHOP?
No...
I couldn't FALL a TREE a foot through in a DAY...
so when the WOOD GUARD was made up
he left me OFF.
I was feeling BETTER since getting BACK TO DUTY
but a COUPLE HOURS of DRILL
made me VERY TIRED
and I could LIFT BUT LITTLE on account of my LAME BACK.

# TENTMATES

JONAS had got WELL OVER his attack of JAUNDICE and was now HEAVIER and LOOKING BETTER than I had ever SEEN him.

We were TOGETHER all the time ....

and at NIGHT we SLEPT together.

I had TWO RUBBER BLANKETS and THREE WOOLEN ones

So we put the RUBBER BLANKETS on the BOTTOM of the BUNK

and JONAS spread his WOOLEN ONES for us to LAY on.

This left MY three woolen blankets to put over US

So we SLEPT as COMFORTABLE as need be

while in the DAYTIME the STOVE kept the tent nice and WARM.

*The* CIVIL WAR DIARY *of* FREEMAN COLBY | **247**

## STOCKADING

While the GOOD WEATHER HELD, we made USE of it....

We CUT TREES into SIX FOOT lengths,

SPLIT the LOGS as THIN as we could

and SET the SLABS thus made

in a TRENCH dug JUST WHERE the EDGE of the TENT would come,

BURYING the lower ends TWO FEET in the ground.

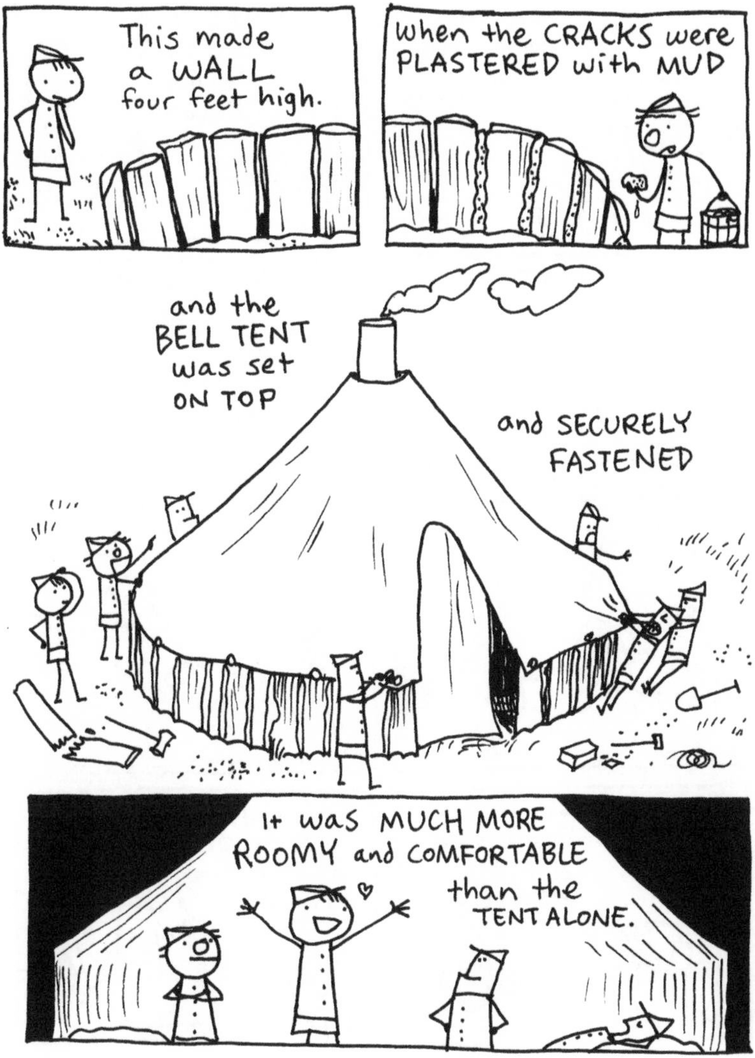

This made a WALL four feet high.
when the CRACKS were PLASTERED with MUD
and the BELL TENT was set ON TOP
and SECURELY FASTENED
It was MUCH MORE ROOMY and COMFORTABLE than the TENT ALONE.

# SHAM FIGHT

On the morning of JANUARY 6

the BATTERY and CAVALRY of our BRIGADE

had a SHAM FIGHT.

We jokingly called it:

The Second Great Battle of Poolsville.

The CAVALRY took the Battery

with the LOSS of ONE MAN'S COAT,

the HAIR which was BURNED OFF one side of his HORSE,

and the BREAKING of a SWORD in the attack.

On the side of the DEFENSE

a GUNNER was INJURED by a BLANK CARTRIDGE.

He was STANDING about THREE FEET from the MUZZLE of his own CANNON

when it WENT OFF.

LUCKILY he was a little TO ONE SIDE

but one of his ARMS was BROKEN in TWO PLACES

and ALL the CLOTHES were BLOWN OFF his SHOULDER and breast.

# LUCKY SOLDIER

About NOON it commenced to RAIN

and BID FAIR for a HARD STORM

but NO amount of RAIN could DAMP MY SPIRITS that day

for I had FIVE LETTERS,

a BIRTHDAY PRESENT,

and one of the BEST BOXES that had EVER come into camp.

I certainly thought myself a LUCKY SOLDIER.

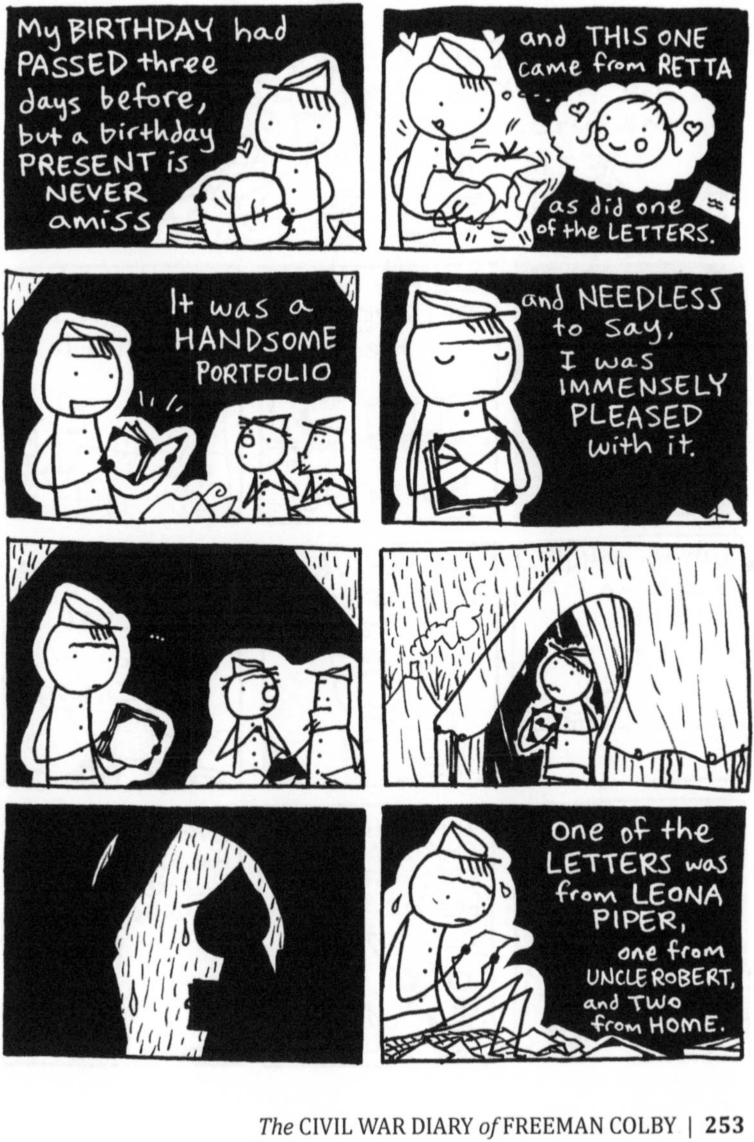
My BIRTHDAY had PASSED three days before, but a birthday PRESENT is NEVER amiss
and THIS ONE came from RETTA
as did one of the LETTERS.
It was a HANDSOME PORTFOLIO
and NEEDLESS to say, I was IMMENSELY PLEASED with it.
One of the LETTERS was from LEONA PIPER, one from UNCLE ROBERT, and TWO from HOME.

Two or three days later there came a PERFECT DELUGE of BOXES for the BOYS.

Nearly EVERY ONE of them had ONE

but they had been SHIPPED to ARRIVE at CHRISTMASTIME

and had been DELAYED on the way

SO LONG

that ALL the FOOD was SPOILED

while MINE had come RIGHT ALONG

and ARRIVED in PERFECT CONDITION.

Not an EGG was BROKEN or a PIE MOULDED.

EVERYTHING I had asked for WAS THERE

and several CHRISTMAS PRESENTS besides.

Even some of the NEIGHBORS had REMEMBERED ME with Christmas GIFTS.

# WEAK AND SICK BUT HAPPY TO BE HOME

Hardly a DAY passed but some of the BOYS asked me about NEWTON...

I was NO LESS ANXIOUS as MAIL after MAIL came

but NO LETTER from HIM or any NEWS of him from HOME.

But AT LAST on Jan. 16 I got a LETTER from NELLIE

telling me he had GOT THERE WEAK and SICK but HAPPY to be HOME ONCE MORE.

He would WRITE TO ME, she said, when he had RESTED UP A LITTLE.

This was GOOD NEWS INDEED...

A few days later, HE wrote telling me what had HAPPENED to him since he had LAST WRITTEN Dec. 2.

# NEWTON'S STORY

He WROTE that he had received the BEST OF CARE at the HOSPITAL

but NONE TOO MUCH to EAT.

The only FULL MEAL he had while he was there was on CHRISTMAS DAY

When ALL the PATIENTS who were ABLE to Eat at all were given THEIR FILL of:

chicken! turkey! bread! PIE! doughnuts! COFFEE!

—a HOLIDAY FEAST indeed.

As fast as the PATIENTS recovered sufficiently enough to TRAVEL

they were SENT AWAY to make ROOM for OTHERS

who were CONSTANTLY ARRIVING from the FIELDS and CAMPS.

SOME were DISCHARGED.

some went HOME on FURLOUGH

and MANY were sent to PHILADELPHIA or BALTIMORE

for further TREATMENT.

He made some FRIENDS among the PATIENTS NEAR him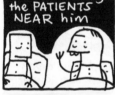

but it was ONLY for a FEW DAYS that they would BE THERE

and then

their COTS would be OCCUPIED by OTHERS

and still OTHERS.

HE STAYED longer than MOST of them.

He made INQUIRIES about getting a DISCHARGE

but there was NO ONE at hand to really DO anything about it ...

and he received LITTLE encouragement,

so he seemed FARTHER THAN EVER

from ANY chance of GOING HOME...

The TREATMENT had but LITTLE EFFECT

and his COUGH was still SO BAD

he could only SLEEP a LITTLE WHILE at a time ...

He MISSED the boys of COMPANY K

and grew every week more HOMESICK.

But on Dec. 22 PARKER RICHARDSON called to see him

and told him of MEETING ME at Poolsville

and what he was PLANNING to DO for him.

After some LITTLE TALK

he went to SEE the WARD SURGEON, Dr. Thompson,

and later the HEAD DOCTOR of the hospital.

He seemed PLEASED with what they had to SAY of the case

and WENT AWAY PROMISING to DO what he COULD for NEWTON at the WAR DEPARTMENT to get him a DISCHARGE.

TWO DAYS later the HEAD SURGEON came and EXAMINED him.

He SOUNDED his LUNGS

and ASKED him A LOT of questions

but WENT AWAY without giving ANY HINT

as to the OPINION he had formed.

This left NEWTON in a FINE STATE of UNCERTAINTY

but DR. THOMPSON, on his FIRST ROUND of the ward,

TOLD HIM that he would GET his DISCHARGE all right.

This was on CHRISTMAS EVE

and the NEWS seemed to be in KEEPING with the TIME

but EVEN THEN he did not feel PERFECTLY SURE of it

as he felt it POSSIBLE they might be PUTTING HIM OFF...

When THEY really DID NOT KNOW whether it was SO or NOT.

THE DOUBT was not reassuring

but he TRIED to be CHEERFUL.

and WAIT

as PATIENTLY

as POSSIBLE.

It was not until the morning of JAN. 1, 1863,

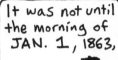

when the DISCHARGE PAPERS were ACTUALLY put in his HAND,

that his DOUBTS were REPLACED

by the GLAD CERTAINTY of SOON GOING HOME!

He was very WEAK

but with the AID of many HELPING HANDS on the ROAD

he reached HENNIKER a week later

TIRED but HAPPY at being HOME AT LAST.

FATHER and MOTHER WELCOMED him like a prodigal RETURNED.

Indeed, I think he FELT like one—

at least as far as MOTHER'S COOKING was concerned.

I ANSWERED at once, telling him how GLAD I was that he was BACK again and giving him the NEWS of the REGIMENT.

We CONTINUED to WRITE to each other

and I soon NOTICED the REST of the family were NOT sending me so MANY LETTERS

and I was NOT getting so MUCH NEWS as BEFORE his return.

NEWTON'S letters were NOT very FREQUENT or REGULAR

for he ALWAYS had TOO MUCH BUSINESS on hand...

so after a time I commenced to feel myself NEGLECTED by them ALL

and WROTE to MOTHER and FATHER asking them to send me ALL THE NEWS as before...

and with their LETTERS

and an occasional MIRROR or DEMOCRAT that they SENT me

I was kept FAIRLY WELL INFORMED on the HOME HAPPENINGS...

# WATCHES

 I was always HANDY with TOOLS

and had done a little work on WATCHES before I enlisted.

So while we were STILL ENCAMPED at BOXFORD (MA)

and getting our FIRST drill work,

I commenced to REPAIR WATCHES for some of the boys.

IT WAS a VERY DIFFERENT BUSINESS THEN from what it is NOW in these days of MACHINE-MADE watches and DUPLICATE PARTS.
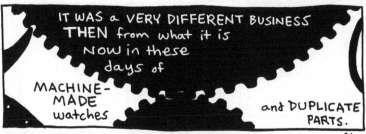

At THAT time there were VERY FEW WATCHES made in AMERICA.

MOST of them were IMPORTED from SWITZERLAND

but a few of the FINEST were made in ENGLAND.

but WHEREVER they came from they were ALL HAND MADE

and DUPLICATE PARTS could only be bought IN THE ROUGH

and had to be WORKED DOWN with LATHE and FILE

to FIT the PARTICULAR WATCH to be REPAIRED.

This was SO MUCH of a JOB

that a BROKEN PART

was often MENDED and made to do FURTHER SERVICE

INSTEAD of being REPLACED with a NEW one.

As it was IMPOSSIBLE for me while I was in the ARMY

to keep ON HAND more than A FEW tools and parts

I CONTRIVED by careful and PAINSTAKING WORK

to DO with THEM MOST of the JOBS that came in my way.

MANY a BROKEN PIVOT

I BORED OUT with my little BOWSTRING DRILL

and put a PIECE cut from a SEWING NEEDLE ......

in its PLACE for the WHEEL to TURN on.

MANY a COG

I FILED and DOVETAILED into place.

EACH JOB presented a DIFFERENT PROBLEM

to be SOLVED AS BEST I could.

SOME of them were EASY

but for OTHERS

I had to MAKE SPECIAL TOOLS

before I could even COMMENCE on the REAL WORK.

I kept ALL the OLD WATCHES I could get hold of

and once in a WHILE I was ABLE

to USE some PART of the WORKS over AGAIN

But with ALL my CONTRIVING there still remained

an OCCASIONAL JOB I simply COULD NOT DO.

THESE I CARRIED about with me

Until I got an opportunity to SEND them

to a JEWELER named HENDERSON at Concord

to be put in RUNNING ORDER and RETURNED to me.

SOMETIMES I sent them BY MAIL

but MORE OFTEN by some NEW HAMPSHIRE MAN

who was going HOME.

It was EVIDENT

that the LONGER we were away

the more CLEANING and REPAIRING there would be to do

So while JONAS and I were WAITING at BOSTON for the regiment to ARRIVE from BOXFORD

I had LAID IN a SUPPLY of HANDS, MAINSPRINGS and CHAINS... also a few more TOOLS.

I put them ALL in my KNAPSACK

which went with the rest as BAGGAGE

and never saw them again

until we had been ON PICKET nearly a WEEK at EDWARD'S FERRY.

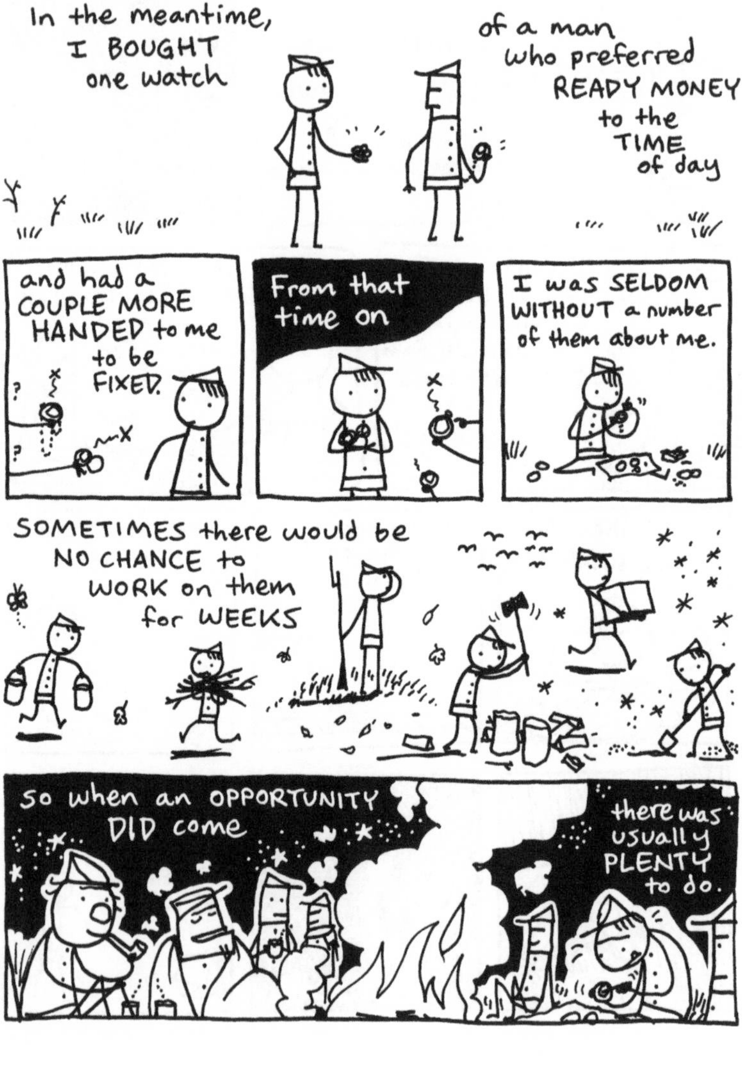
In the meantime, I BOUGHT one watch
of a man who preferred READY MONEY to the TIME of day
and had a COUPLE MORE HANDED to me to be FIXED.
From that time on
I was SELDOM WITHOUT a number of them about me.
SOMETIMES there would be NO CHANCE to WORK on them for WEEKS
so when an OPPORTUNITY DID come
there was usually PLENTY to do.

As NONE of us had seen a DOLLAR of PAY since we ENLISTED, it was NO WONDER that MONEY was SCARCE

but after we went into WINTER QUARTERS

I found that by putting in ALL my SPARE TIME

I could get enough READY CASH

to pay my EXPENSES

and do even MORE work "ON TICK" — to be paid when the PAYMASTER came.

For a TIME, while BUSINESS was GOOD,

I even had THOUGHTS of being ABLE to SAVE ENOUGH MONEY while I was in the ARMY

to REALIZE my AMBITION of TAKING a COURSE at Comer's Commercial College after the WAR was over.

But though my NEEDS were FEW,

PRICES were HIGH and grew HIGHER

So LONG BEFORE the CLOSE of the WAR

My EXPENSES

took ALL the MONEY I could get HOLD of.

# MUD

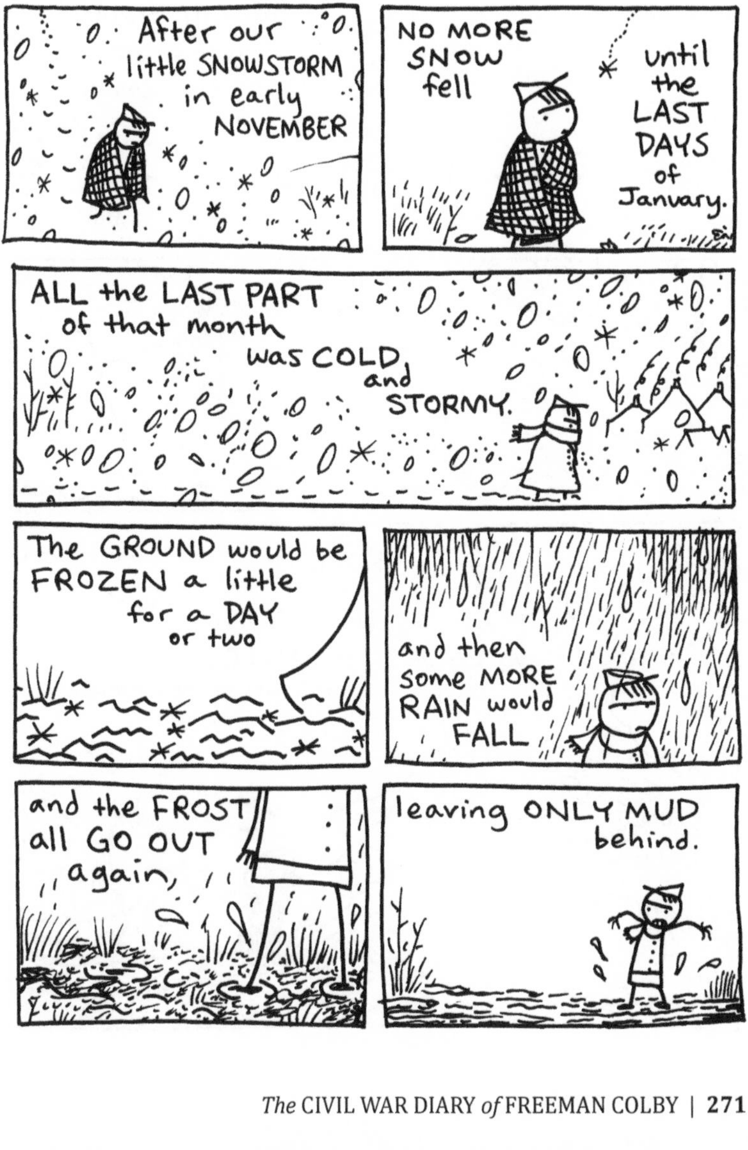

After our little SNOWSTORM in early NOVEMBER
NO MORE SNOW fell
until the LAST DAYS of January.
ALL the LAST PART of that month
was COLD and STORMY.
The GROUND would be FROZEN a little for a DAY or two
and then some MORE RAIN would FALL
and the FROST all GO OUT again,
leaving ONLY MUD behind.

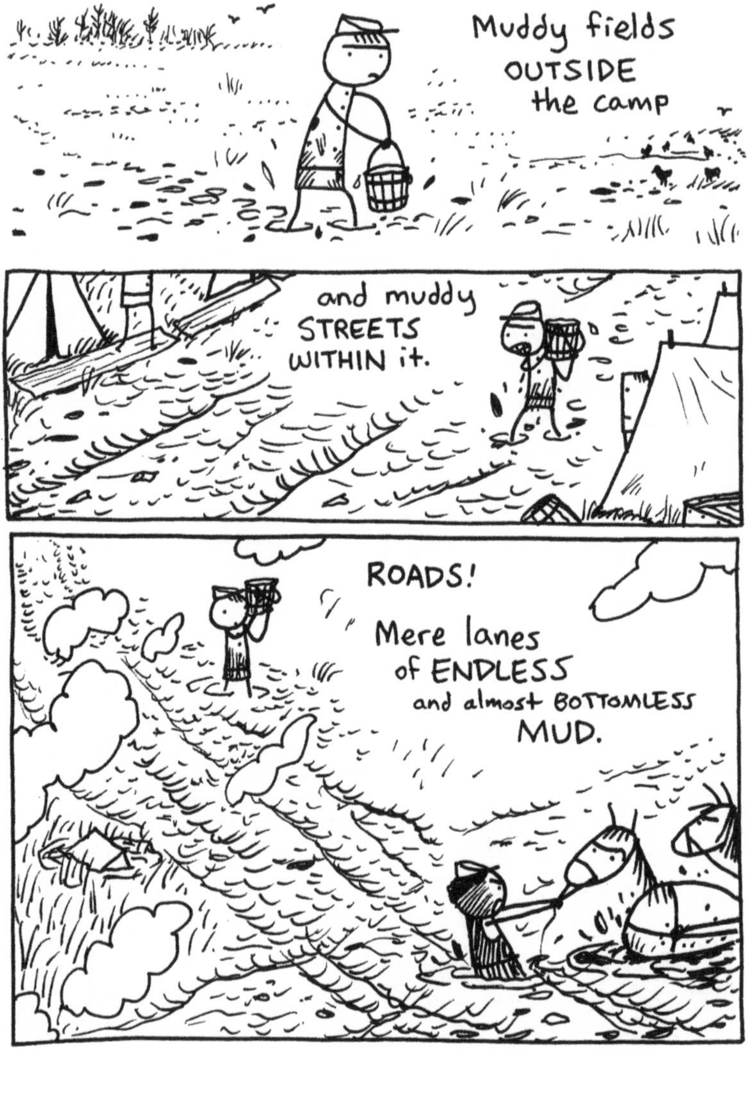
Muddy fields
OUTSIDE
the camp
and muddy
STREETS
WITHIN it.
ROADS!
Mere lanes
of ENDLESS
and almost BOTTOMLESS
MUD.

MULES

To bring our PROVISIONS and SUPPLIES,

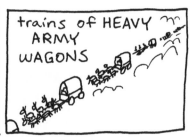
trains of HEAVY ARMY WAGONS

TOILED ALONG axle deep in MUD...

DRAWN by strings of MULES harnessed tandem,

WALLOWING to their BELLIES in the COLD, red SLOUGH

and URGED ON by SWEARING DRIVERS

who SPARED neither TONGUE nor LASH

to keep them MOVING

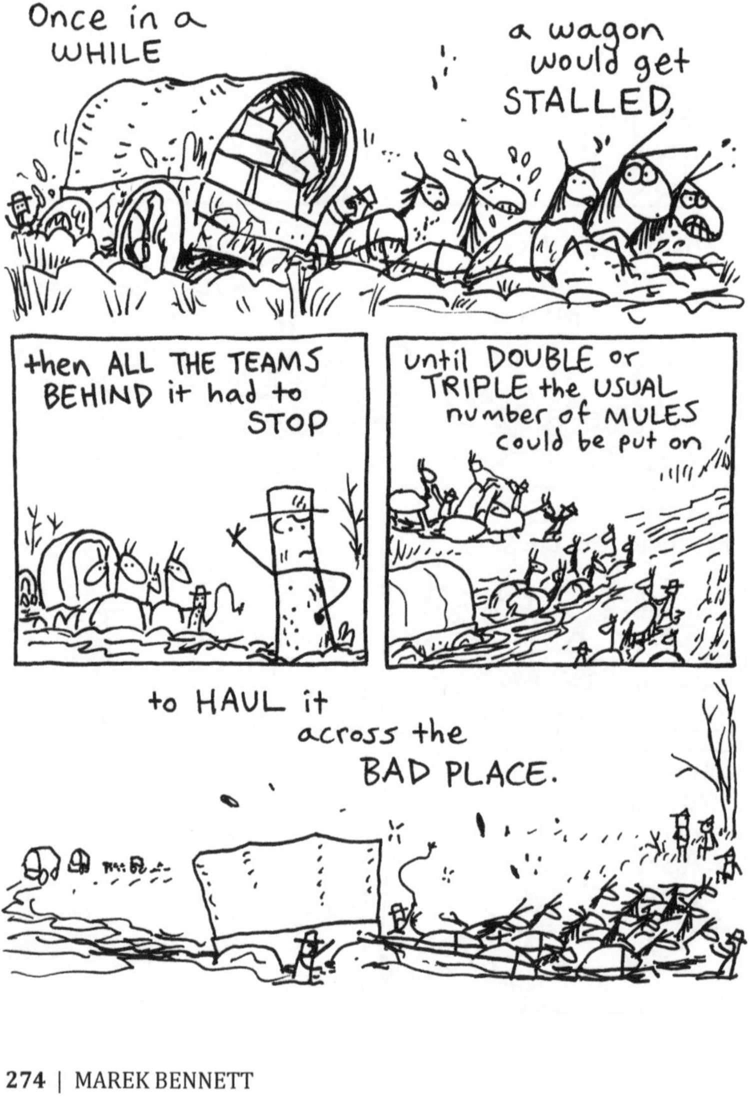
Once in a WHILE
a wagon would get STALLED,
then ALL THE TEAMS BEHIND it had to STOP
until DOUBLE or TRIPLE the USUAL number of MULES could be put on
to HAUL it across the BAD PLACE.

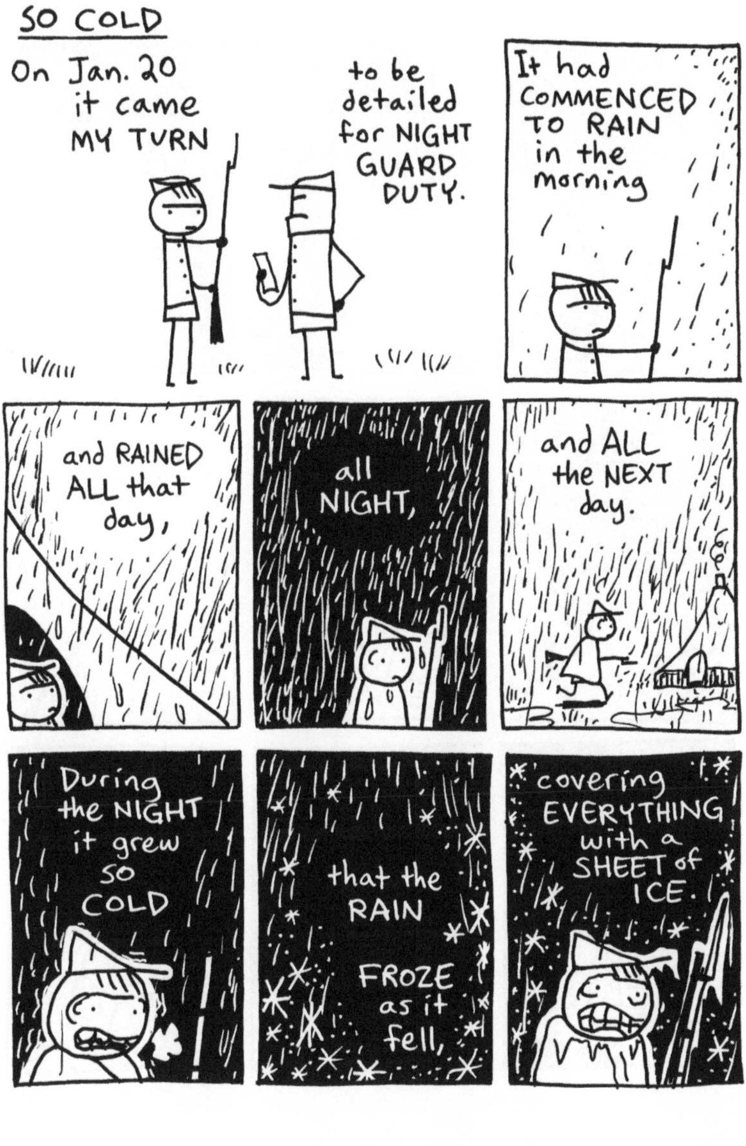
SO COLD
On Jan. 20 it came MY TURN
to be detailed for NIGHT GUARD DUTY.
It had COMMENCED TO RAIN in the morning
and RAINED ALL that day,
all NIGHT,
and ALL the NEXT day.
During the NIGHT it grew SO COLD
that the RAIN
FROZE as it fell,
covering EVERYTHING with a SHEET of ICE.

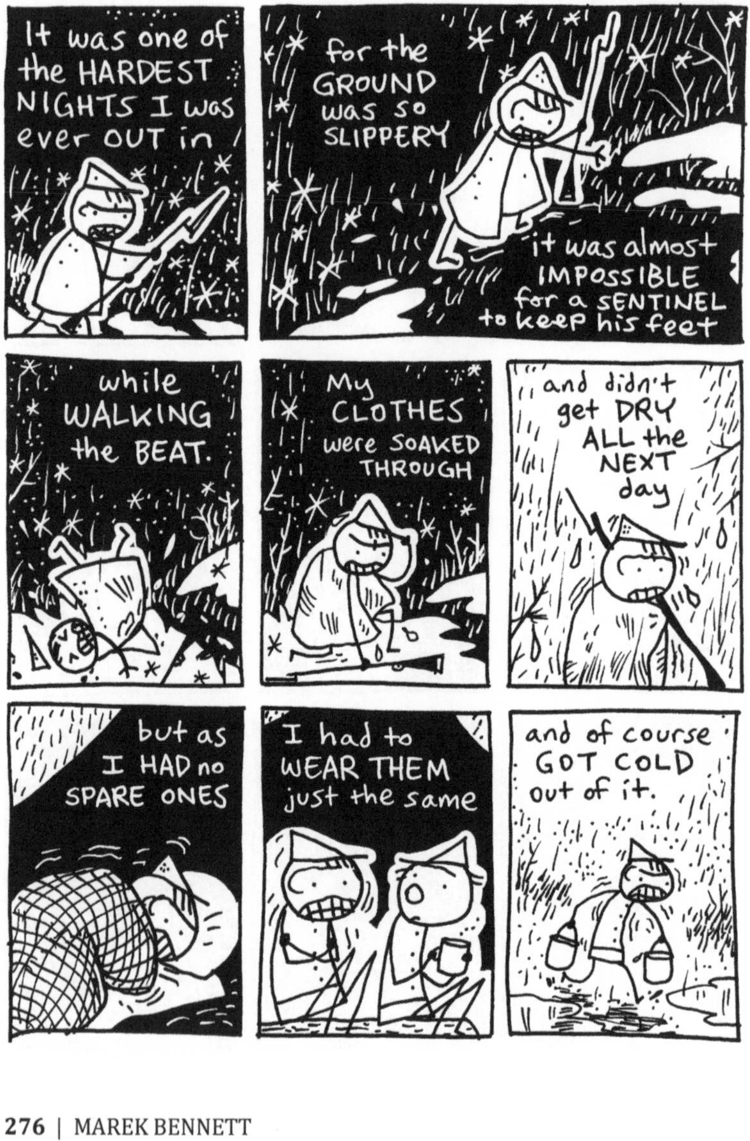
It was one of the HARDEST NIGHTS I was ever OUT in
for the GROUND was so SLIPPERY
it was almost IMPOSSIBLE for a SENTINEL to keep his feet
while WALKING the BEAT.
My CLOTHES were SOAKED THROUGH
and didn't get DRY ALL the NEXT day
but as I HAD no SPARE ONES
I had to WEAR THEM just the same
and of course GOT COLD out of it.

# BURNSIDE

For the balance of JANUARY and well into FEBRUARY the STORMY WEATHER continued,

SNOWING and RAINING alternately.

This made FIELD OPERATIONS very DIFFICULT

but BURNSIDE was making ANOTHER ATTEMPT

to take FREDERICKSBURG.

Possibly he chose THIS TIME

So the REBELS would find it DIFFICULT

to SEND REINFORCEMENTS.

It was HARD ENOUGH for OUR troops to MOVE anyway.

BURNSIDE had taken COMMAND of the Army of the POTOMAC the previous December

when McLELLAN was RETIRED.

Frequent REPORTS and RUMORS of his progress REACHED US

and when it was UNDERSTOOD that part of OUR TROOPS had CROSSED the RIVER above and below the CITY,

the ARTILLERY remaining on THIS side to SHELL the town when all was READY for the ATTACK,

it was ANNOUNCED that WE would be ORDERED OUT to REINFORCE them.

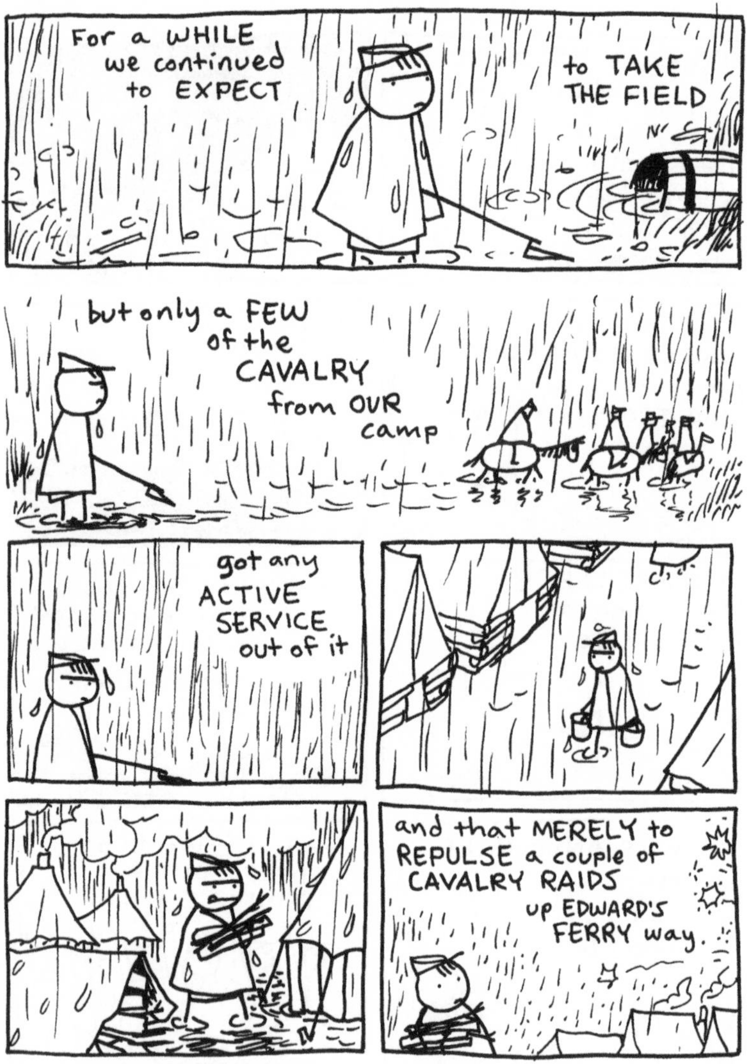
For a WHILE we continued to EXPECT
to TAKE THE FIELD
but only a FEW of the CAVALRY from OUR camp
got any ACTIVE SERVICE out of it
and that MERELY to REPULSE a couple of CAVALRY RAIDS
up EDWARD'S FERRY way.

# BEDDING

It was SO WET EVERYWHERE

that our BEDDING was DAMP all the time

though the RUBBER BLANKETS kept it from actually TOUCHING the GROUND.

So Jonas and I got hold of some BOARDS

and a few STICKS and NAILS

and MADE a BUNK in our TENT

and ANOTHER in the SICK TENT...

which I OCCUPIED for a FEW DAYS

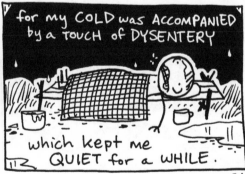

for my COLD was ACCOMPANIED by a TOUCH of DYSENTERY

which kept me QUIET for a WHILE.

~

# SICK LIST

JONAS had a BAD COUGH

but remained ON DUTY.

CAPTAIN RICHARDSON was SICK in the hospital,

also LIEUTENANT DROWN whose ANKLE was growing OUT OF SHAPE.

DR. PARKS the COMPANY SURGEON was SICK with the DYSENTERY in camp

and ALL the DOCTORS had plenty to do.

Just as soon as I could GET ABOUT, I reported for DUTY

but every time I went ON GUARD

I got MORE COLD

and just at the END of this LONG STORMY TIME

when there were SIGNS to be SEEN of the APPROACH of SPRING.

I was TAKEN after coming OFF DUTY, with a bad SORE THROAT

I put on some LINAMENT

which seemed to HELP IT a little for a time

but my LUNGS were soon as SORE as my THROAT

and to SAVE MY LIFE I could NOT draw a LONG BREATH.

At first the DOCTOR had NO MERCY on me

but after SOUNDING my lungs

he ORDERED me to the HOSPITAL.

I stayed there two days and nights

and then I BEGGED SO HARD to be allowed to GO BACK to quarters

that he said I MIGHT

IF I would PROMISE to STAY THERE

and keep OUT of the MUD

I was SHORT OF BREATH for my LUNGS remained very SORE

and at NIGHT I was KEPT AWAKE by long spells of COUGHING

The DOCTOR gave me MURIATE OF IRON

three times a day

and I had PLENTY OF COUGH MEDICINE

but there was LITTLE improvement until the WARMER WEATHER and occasional pleasant SUNNY DAYS of early MARCH.

Then I commenced to GET ABOUT again

but the MONTH was WELL ALONG

before I was ABLE to REPORT for DUTY.

## DREAMS OF HOME

The TIME went very SLOWLY while I was SHUT UP in quarters.

My WATCH REPAIRING helped a little by keeping me OCCUPIED at least PART of the time.

But how I did WISH I could be at HOME

if only long enough to TALK with MOTHER and FATHER and the GIRLS a few minutes

and have a good MEAL with them.

I got to DREAMING of them nearly EVERY night.

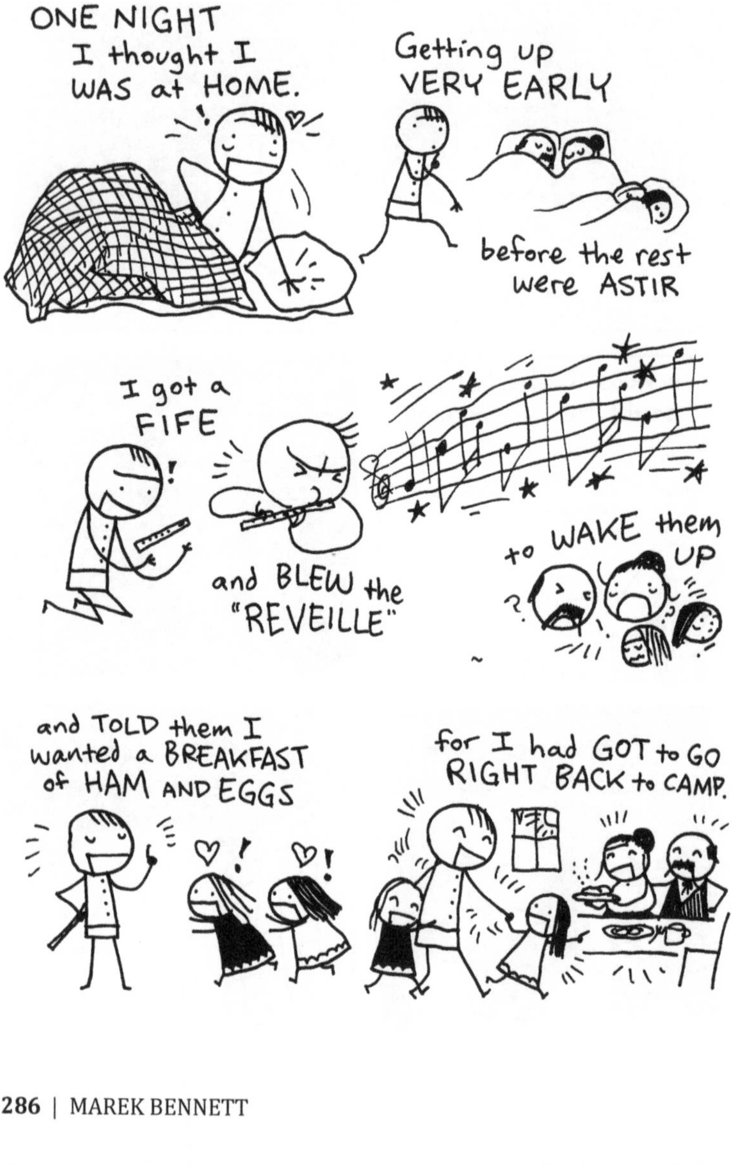
ONE NIGHT I thought I WAS at HOME.
Getting up VERY EARLY
before the rest were ASTIR
I got a FIFE
and BLEW the "REVEILLE"
to WAKE them UP
and TOLD them I wanted a BREAKFAST of HAM AND EGGS
for I had GOT to GO RIGHT BACK to CAMP.

It was all SO REAL

that the SURPRISE CAME when I OPENED my EYES

to see only the DINGY CANVAS and MUD-CHINKED WALLS of the TENT.

The VIVID IMPRESSION of the DREAM remained and was a COMFORT to me

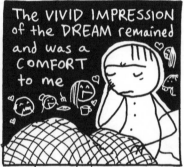

but a GLANCE at my SURROUNDINGS (and particularly at my CLOTHES) was SUFFICIENT to DISPEL any suggestion of the REALITY

for they were QUITE THE SAME as usual.

*The* CIVIL WAR DIARY *of* FREEMAN COLBY | **287**

## CLOTHING

I had the SAME PANTS ON that I had WORN for almost EIGHT MONTHS.

In ALL THAT TIME I had never once had them OFF

except to take a BATH

and WASH my UNDERCLOTHES once in a while.

NATURALLY they were NOT in the BEST of condition

but they were NEARLY WHOLE

and that was MORE than MOST of the boys could say.

We had a STATED ALLOWANCE for CLOTHING and EQUIPMENTS for each of the THREE YEARS of our ENLISTMENT.

For the FIRST YEAR it was $46.00

and I hoped NOT to EXCEED that amount

for whatever we drew OVER that would be taken OUT of our PAY.

EACH ARTICLE was PRICED so we could keep an ACCOUNT

and KNOW just WHEN we had drawn UP TO the ALLOWANCE.

I was HELPED that I had done HARDLY ANY WORK worth speaking of

for the last FOUR MONTHS

and consequently had been VERY EASY on my CLOTHES.

LATER ON when GOLD was at a PREMIUM, the ALLOWANCE was increased to $100.65 for the FIRST YEAR,

$62.54 for the SECOND YEAR,

and $86.93 for the THIRD YEAR.

(TOTAL = $250.12)

# TOO LATE

ONE DAY a young fellow TOOK COLD

from STANDING GUARD in the RAIN and MUD.

when he REPORTED SICK,

the DOCTOR said he was ALL RIGHT

and ordered him BACK TO WORK

He PROTESTED,

but it was NO USE.

Then he SAUCED him—

Which made the DOCTOR SO ANGRY

that he persisted in REFUSING to TREAT him

until it was TOO LATE for ANY treatment to be of USE.

When he was finally DISCOVERED one morning

to be TOO ILL and WEAK to do DUTY

he was taken to the HOSPITAL TENT

and DIED within a WEEK.

~

This was only ONE

of several INSTANCES

somewhat similar

well KNOWN about the CAMP.

Is it any WONDER

that we felt ILLNESS to be PERILOUS under such CONDITIONS

and came to DOUBT the VALUE and EFFICIENCY of the MEDICAL SERVICE

in the EARLY part of the war?

# PLAYING OFF

Our **HEAD SURGEON's** name was **MITCHELL**.

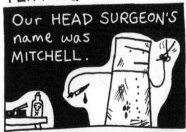

He had **CHARGE** of the **SICK TENTS**.

and from **TIME to TIME** nearly **ALL of us** had **EXPERIENCE** of the way they were **RUN**.

While he kept **SOME** men **OUT** who were **REALLY SICK**,

**TOO MANY** were **ALLOWED** to **STAY** there

when they were **MORE FIT** for **DUTY**

than most of **THOSE**

who were on **SOME DETAIL** or other nearly **EVERY DAY.**

*The* CIVIL WAR DIARY *of* FREEMAN COLBY | **293**

THEY were WELL ENOUGH

EXCEPT when the DOCTOR was around.

SOME of them became ADEPTS at PLAYING OFF,

like JACK DOWNING, whose HEARING was FAILING.

Jack even HOPED to get a DISCHARGE out of it

CLANG
CLANG
CLANG
CLANG

IF he could KEEP IT UP long enough.

# SETTLED

NO ONE would GIVE the GAME away
but there was a GENERAL CHUCKLE went around

when the DOCTOR went into the SICK TENT of CAPTAIN HUNT'S COMPANY one day

and FOUND a couple of them FRYING BEEFSTEAK

He put them in the GUARDHOUSE.

Captain Hunt took them OUT.

The DOCTOR SAW them outside a little later

and put them BACK IN AGAIN.

Then he WENT to the CAPTAIN and ASKED him what he MEANT

by LETTING the MEN GO after HE had locked them in the GUARDHOUSE.

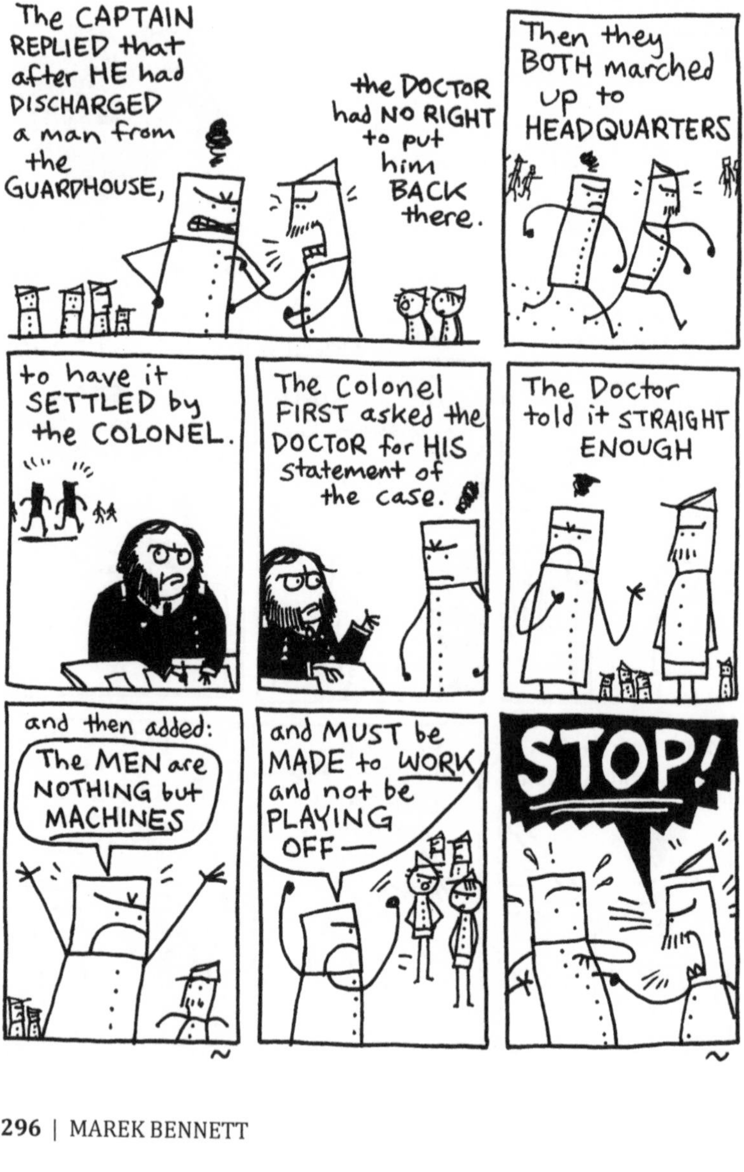

The CAPTAIN REPLIED that after HE had DISCHARGED a man from the GUARDHOUSE,
the DOCTOR had NO RIGHT to put him BACK there.
Then they BOTH marched up to HEADQUARTERS
to have it SETTLED by the COLONEL.
The Colonel FIRST asked the DOCTOR for HIS statement of the case.
The Doctor told it STRAIGHT ENOUGH
and then added:
The MEN are NOTHING but MACHINES
and MUST be MADE to WORK and not be PLAYING OFF —
STOP!

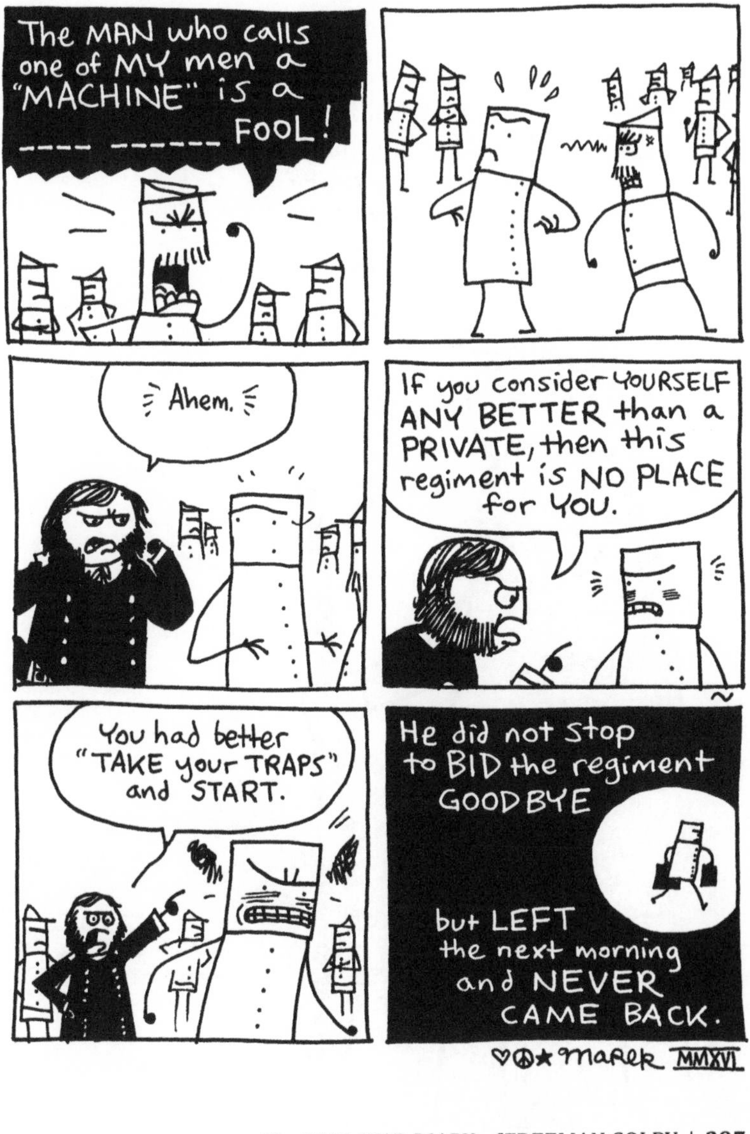
The MAN who calls one of MY men a "MACHINE" is a ---- ------ FOOL!
Ahem.
If you consider YOURSELF ANY BETTER than a PRIVATE, then this regiment is NO PLACE for YOU.
You had better "TAKE your TRAPS" and START.
He did not stop to BID the regiment GOODBYE
but LEFT the next morning and NEVER CAME BACK.
marek MMXVI

Freeman Colby's
adventures continue in:
*The Civil War Diary
of Freeman Colby,
VOLUME 2*

# APPENDIX.
## GALLERY *of* SCENES.

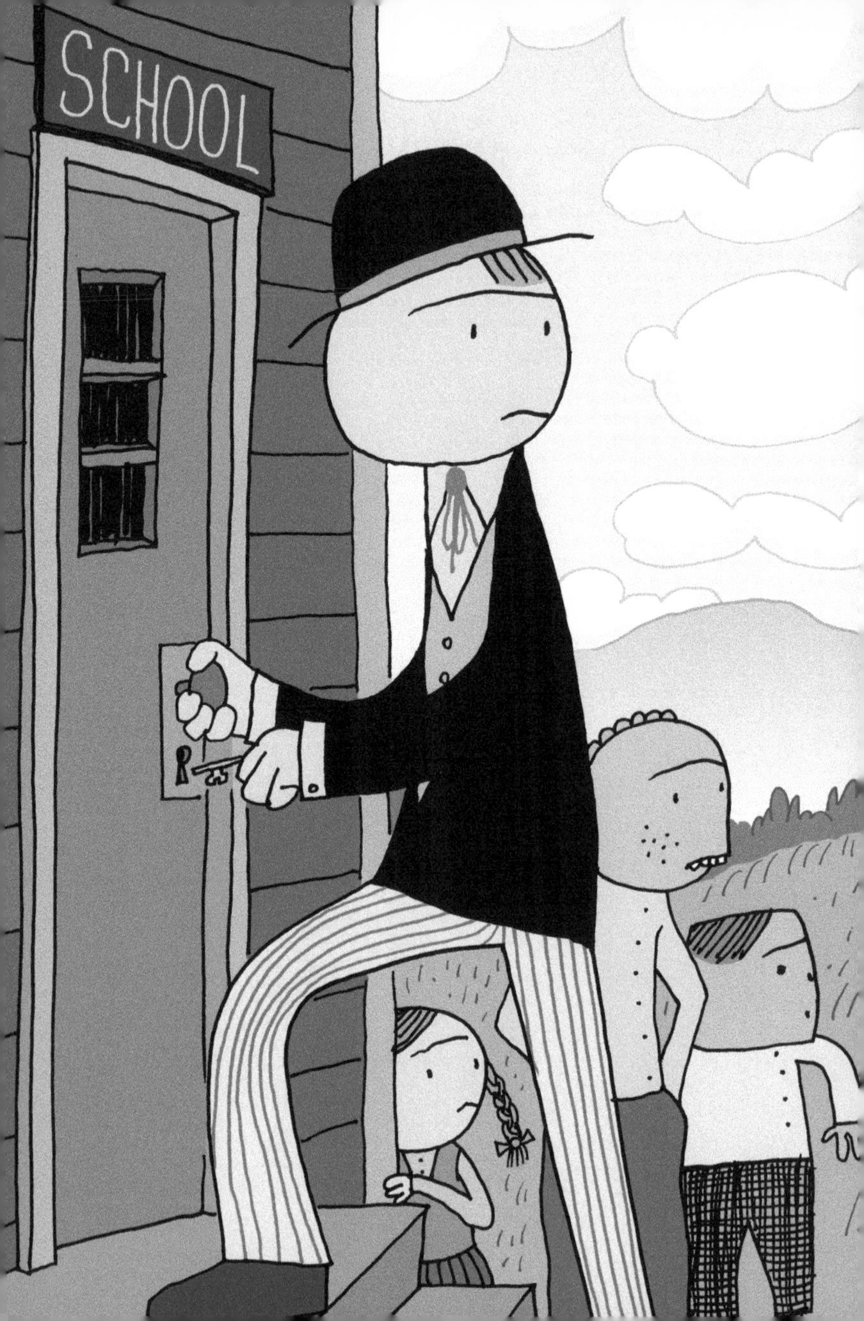
SCHOOL

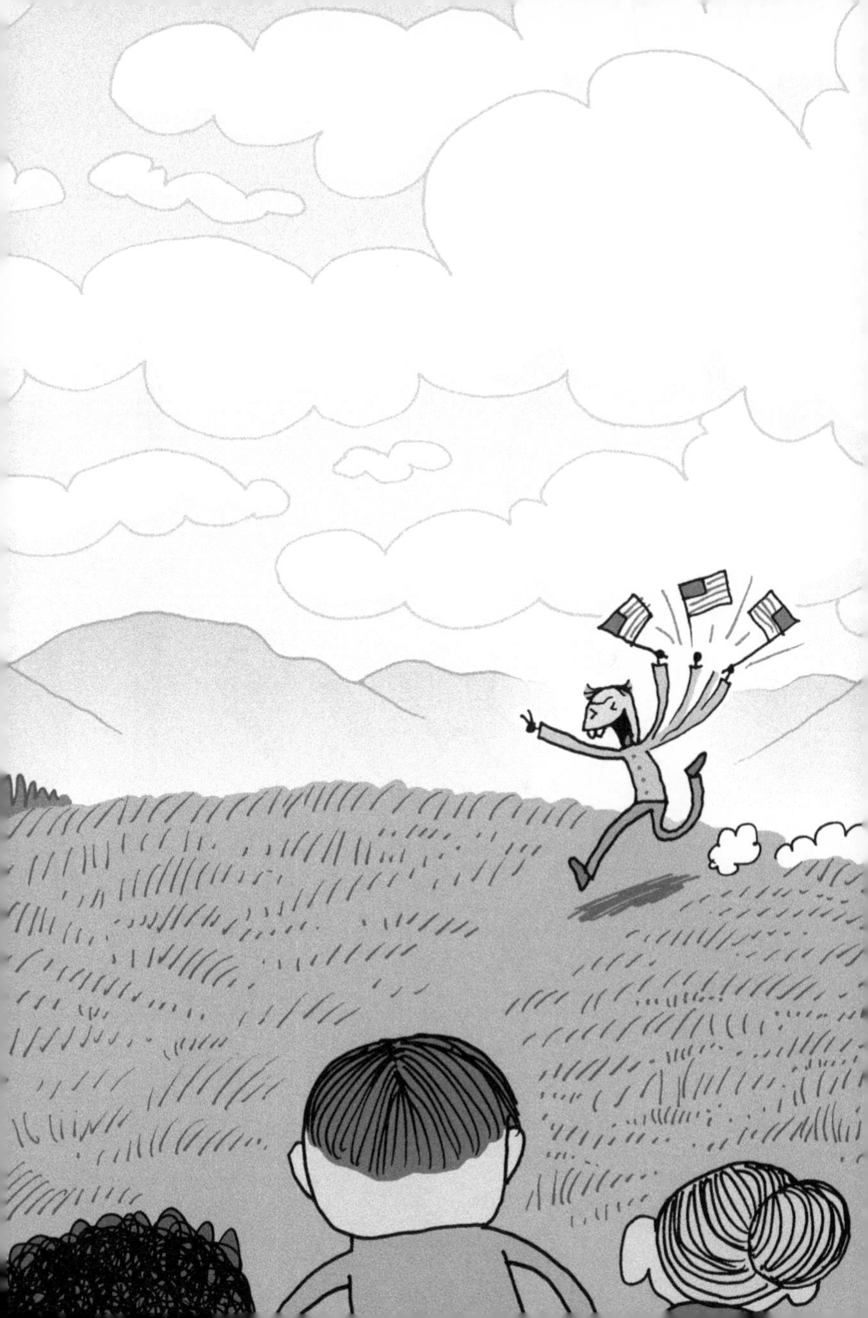

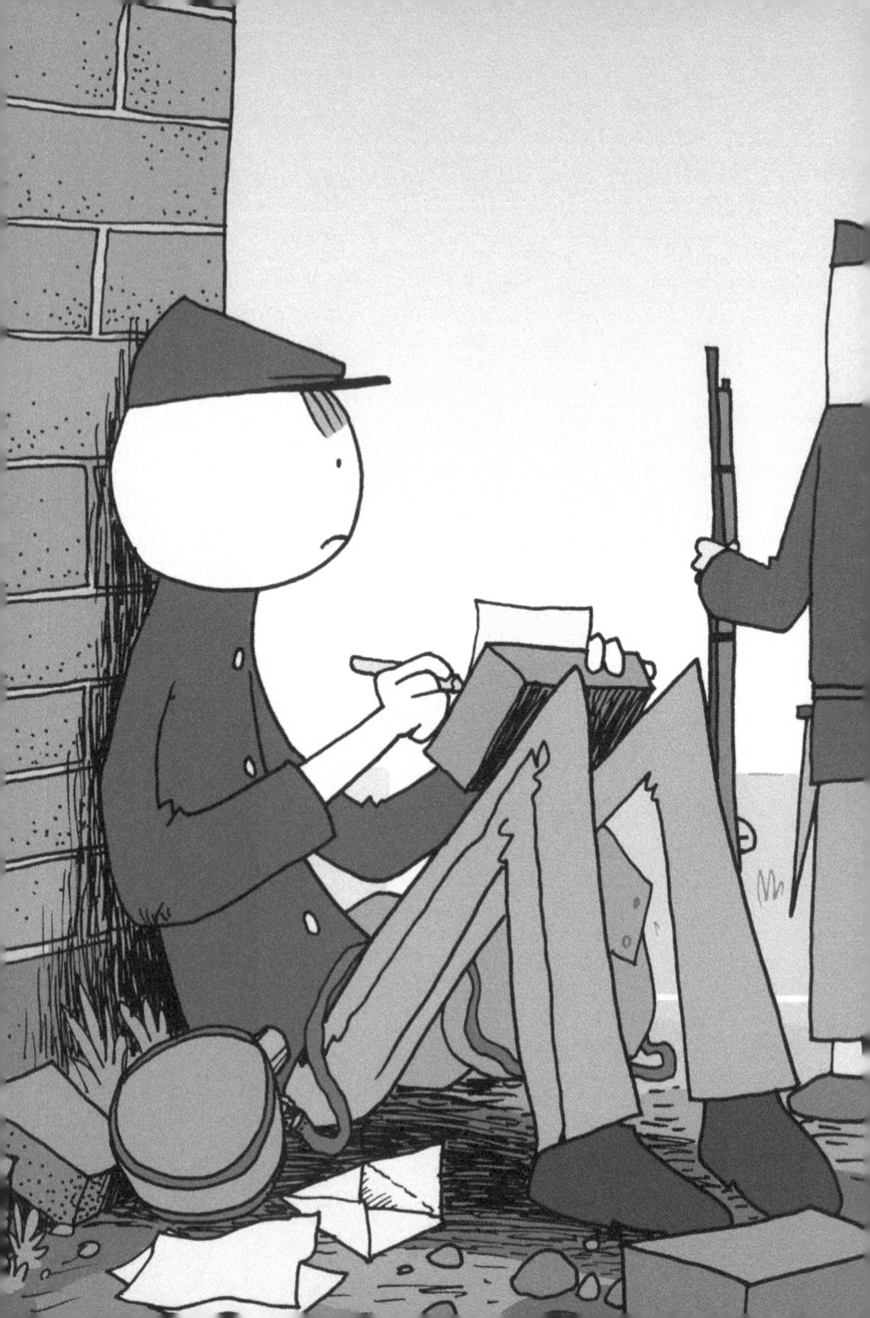

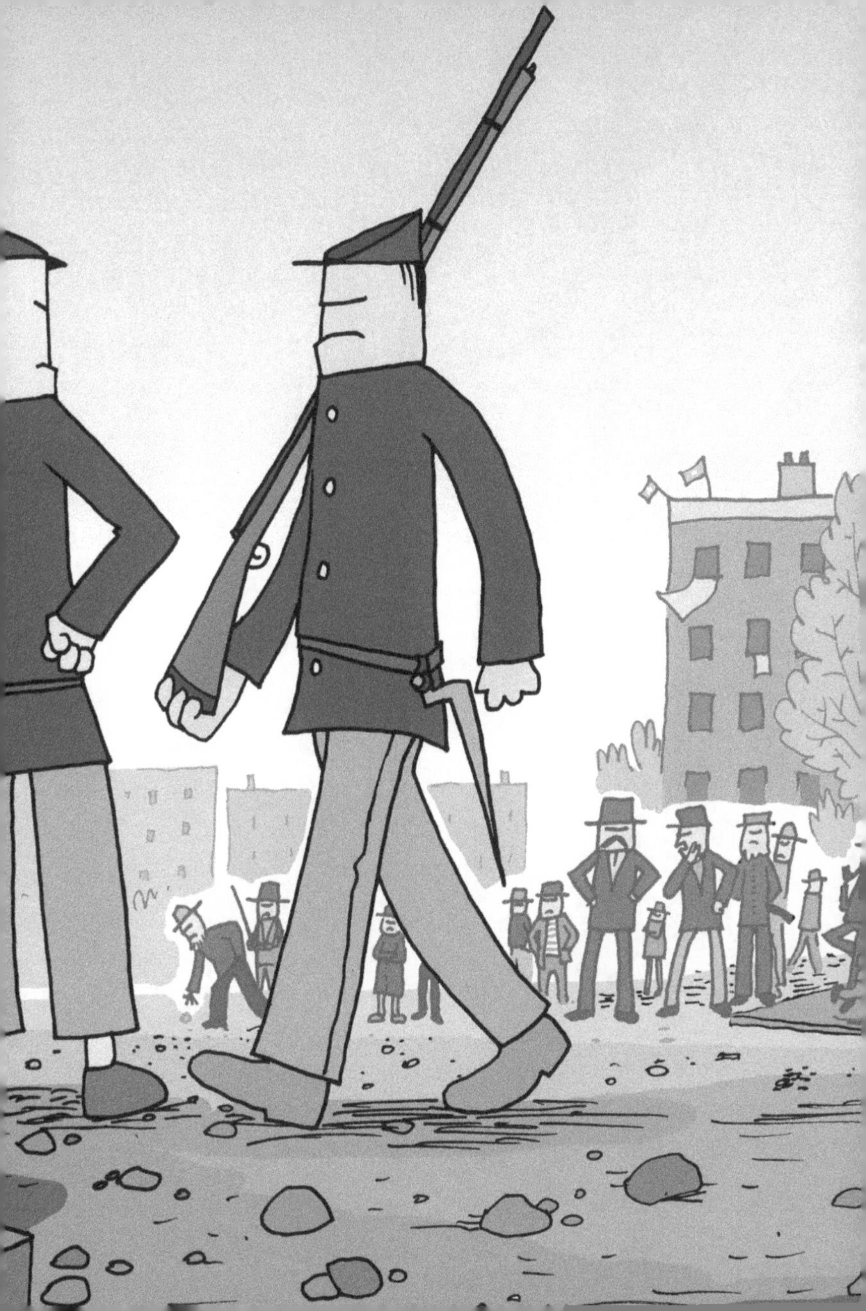

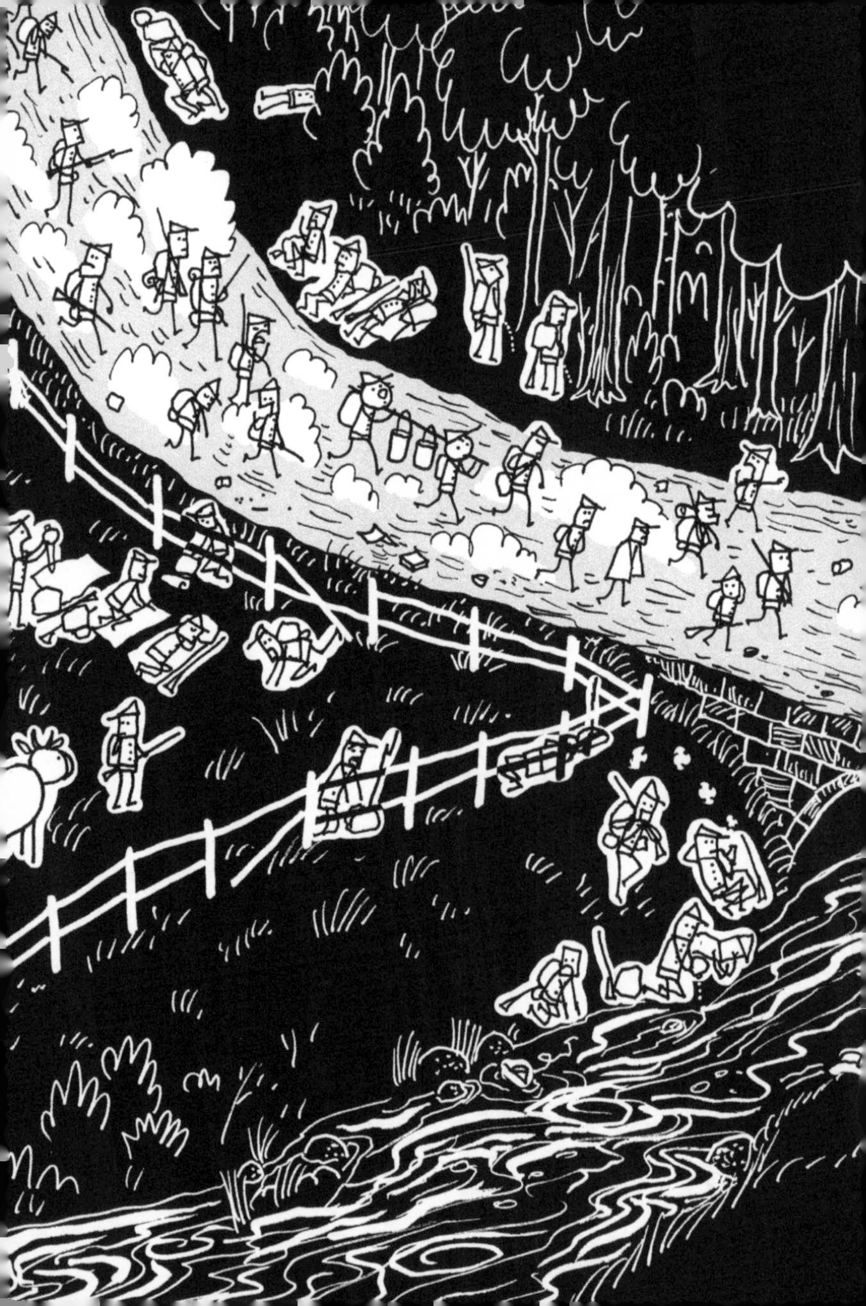

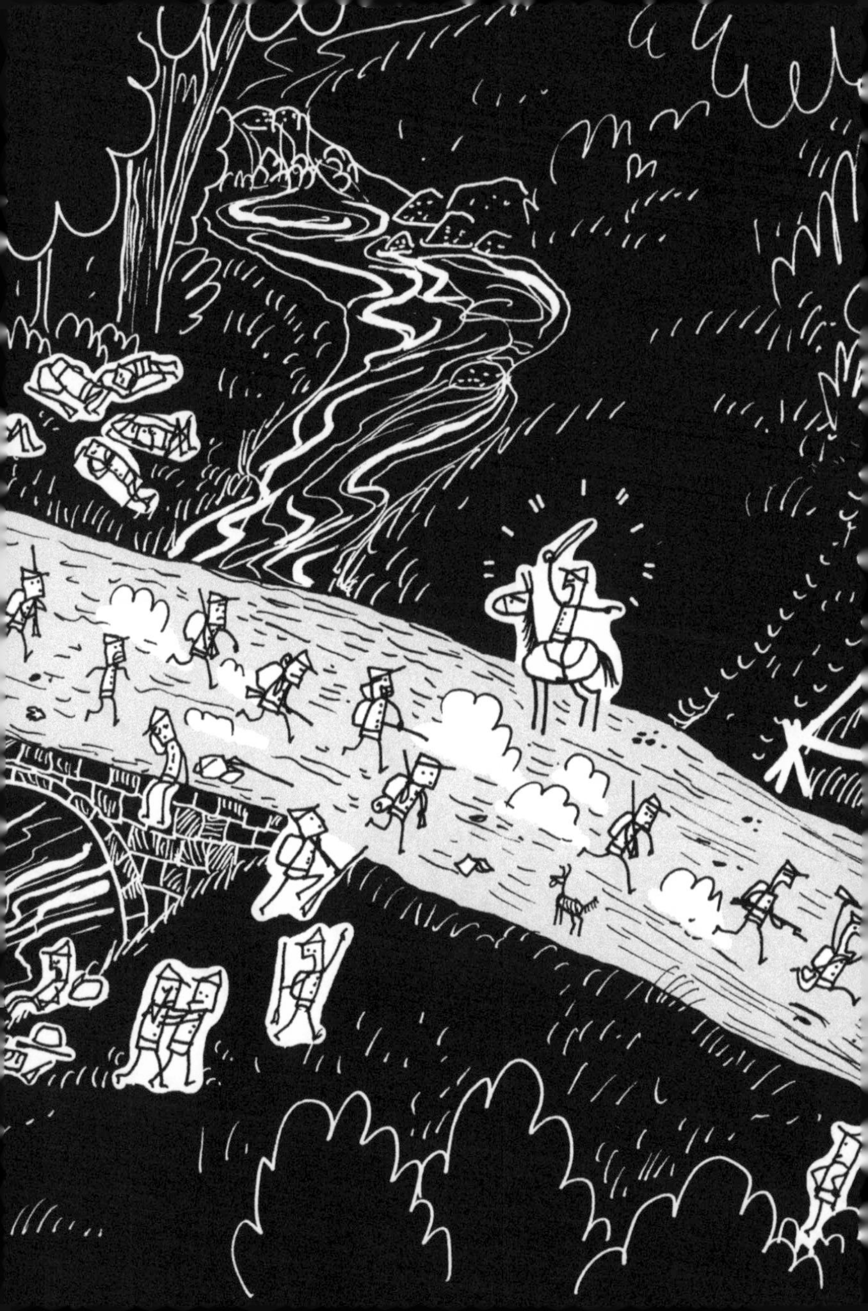

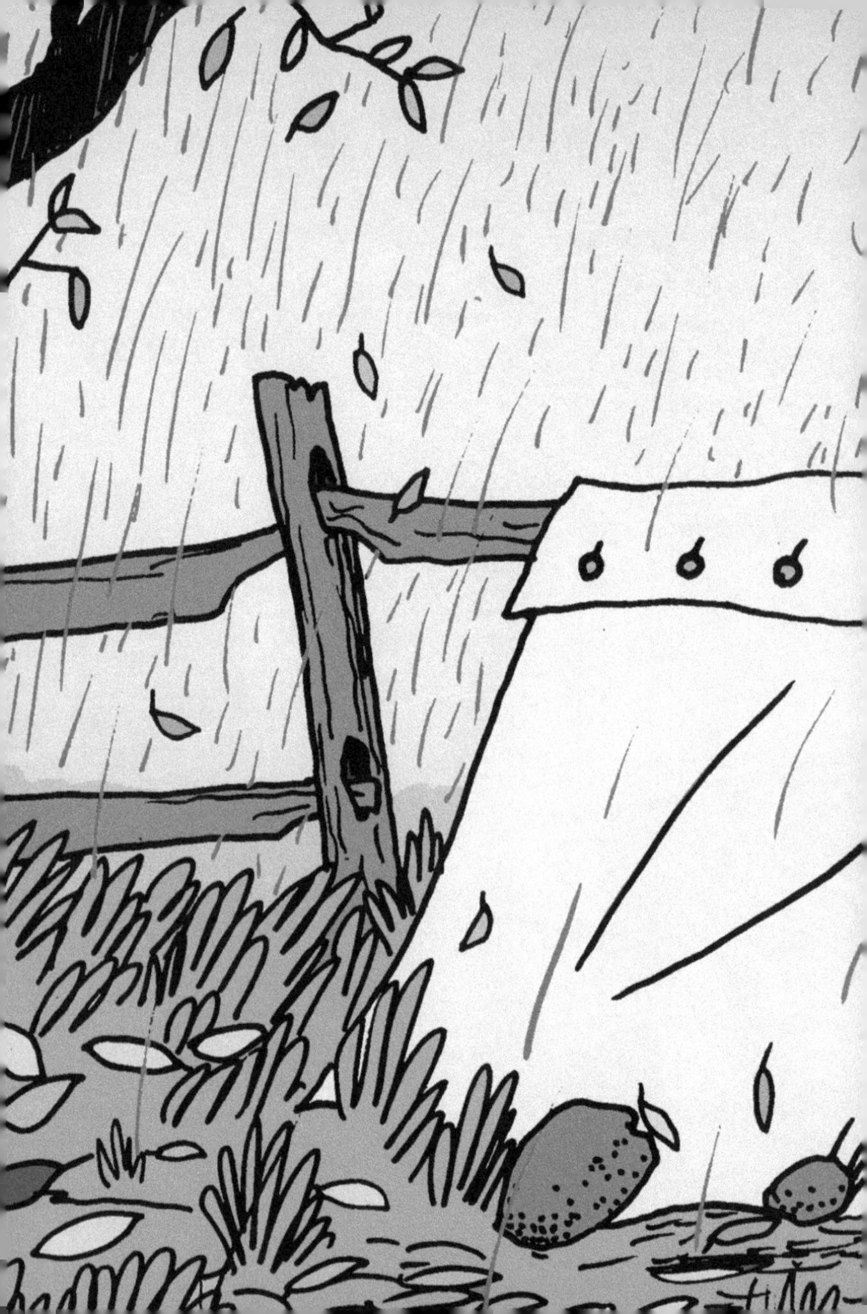

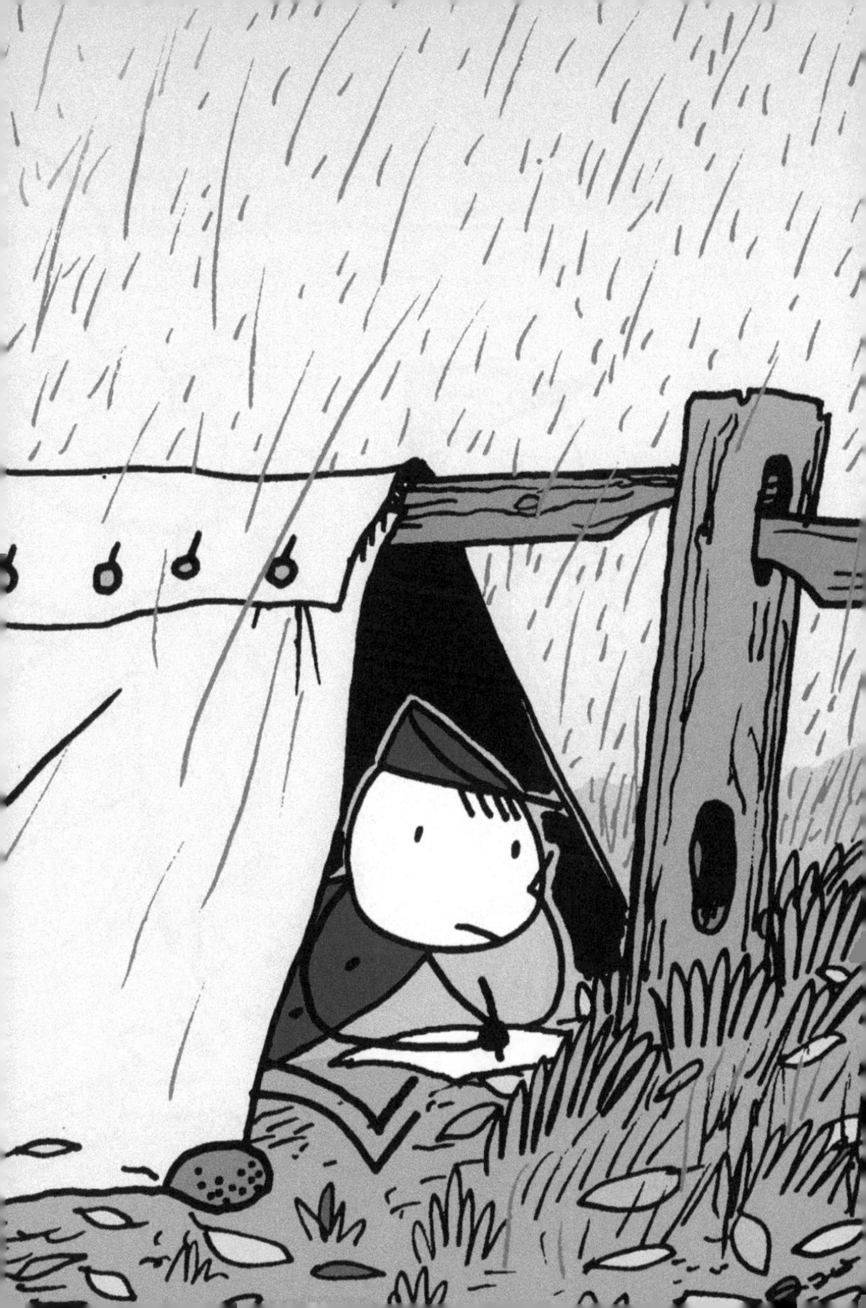

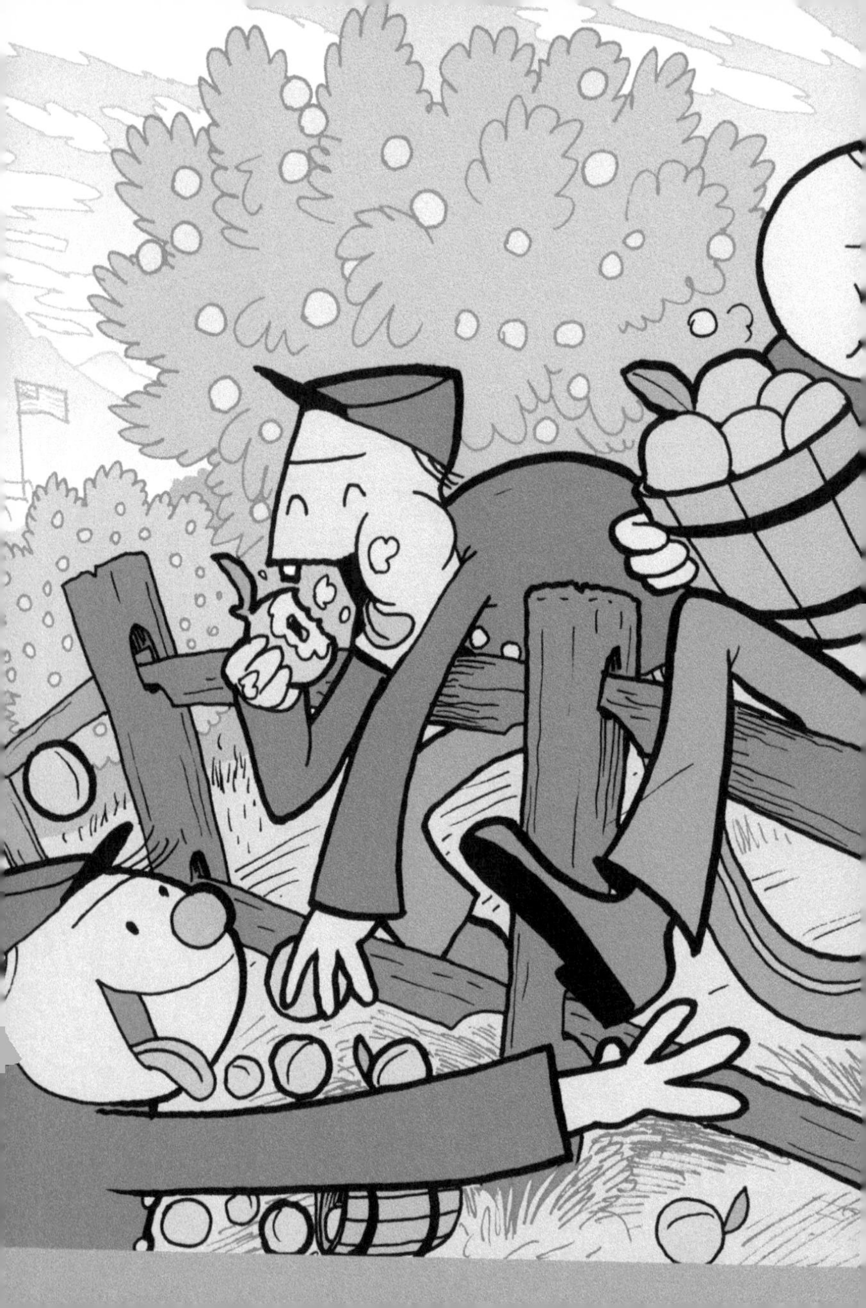

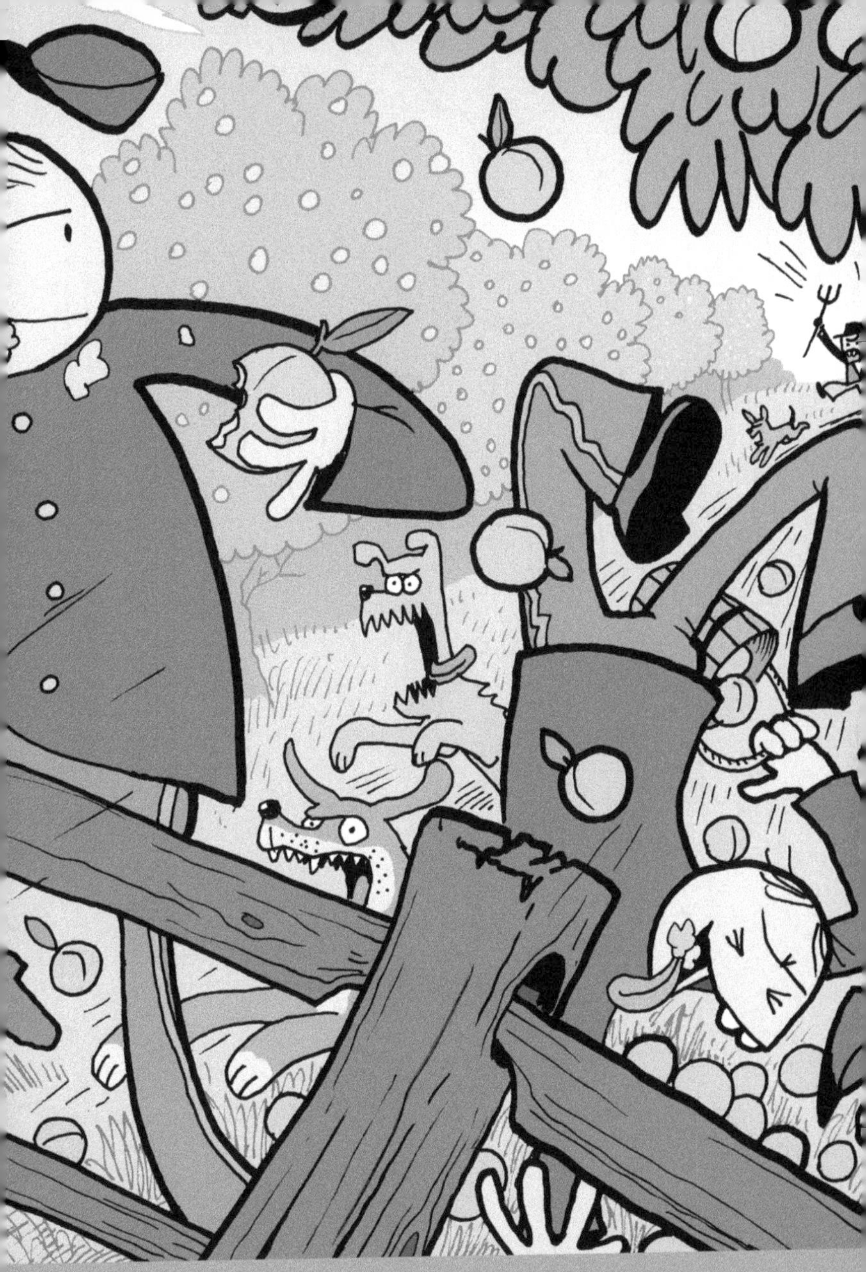

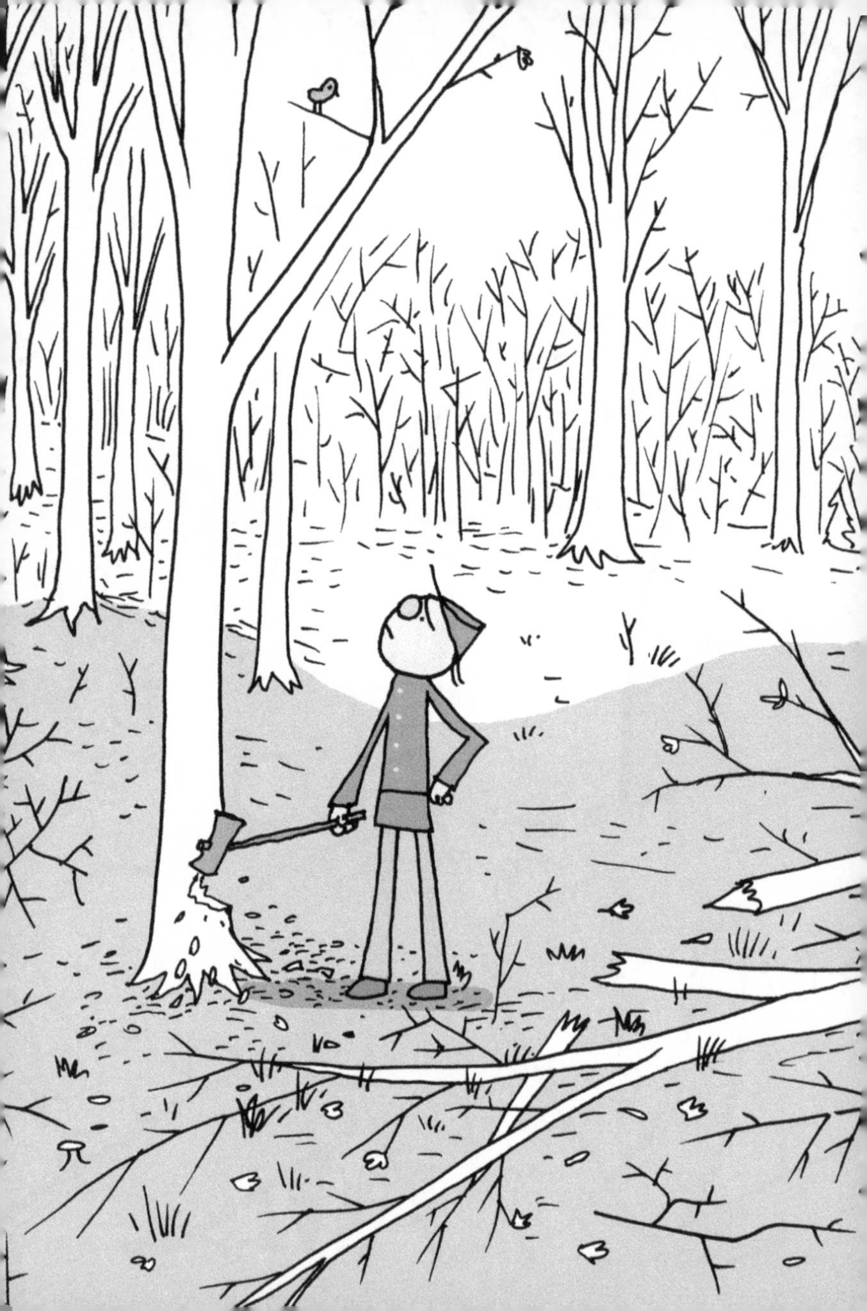

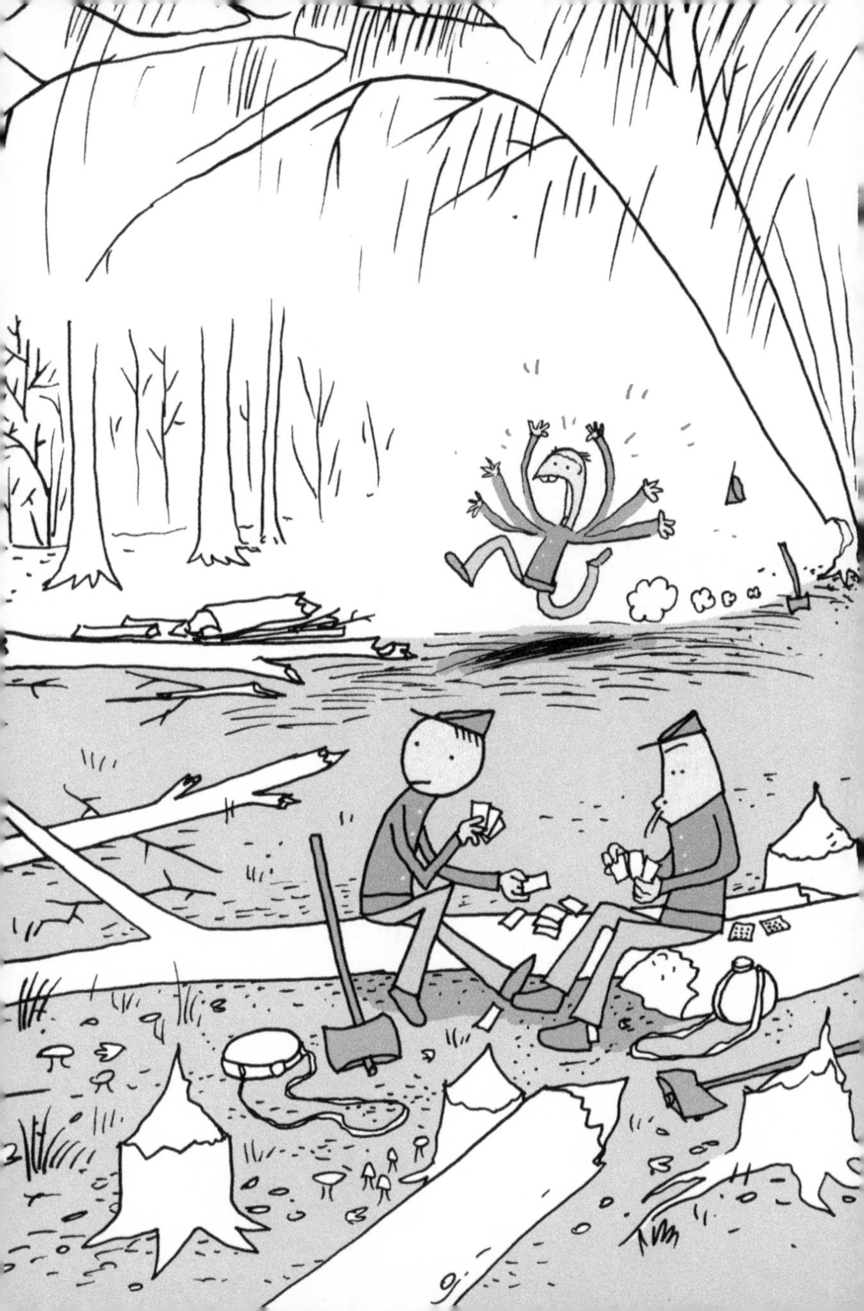

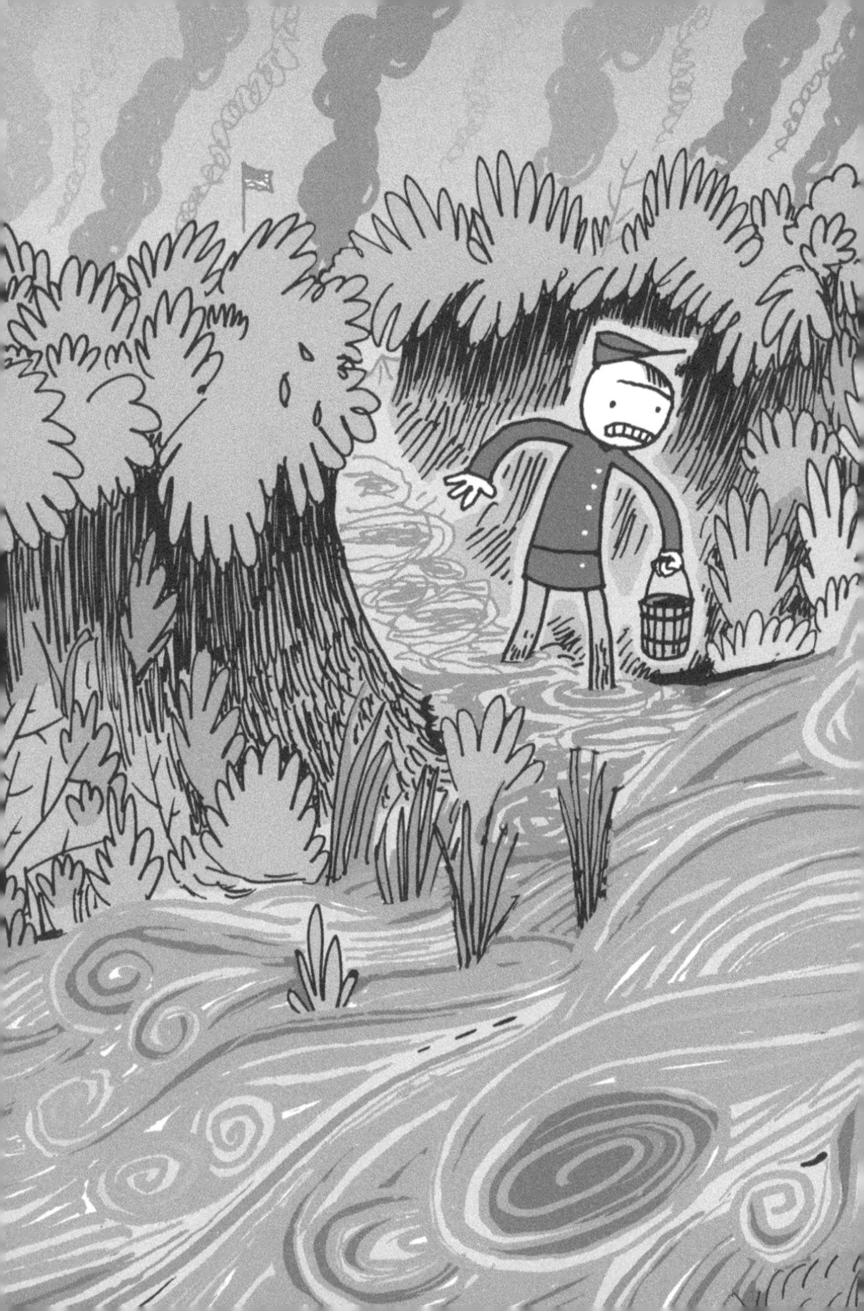

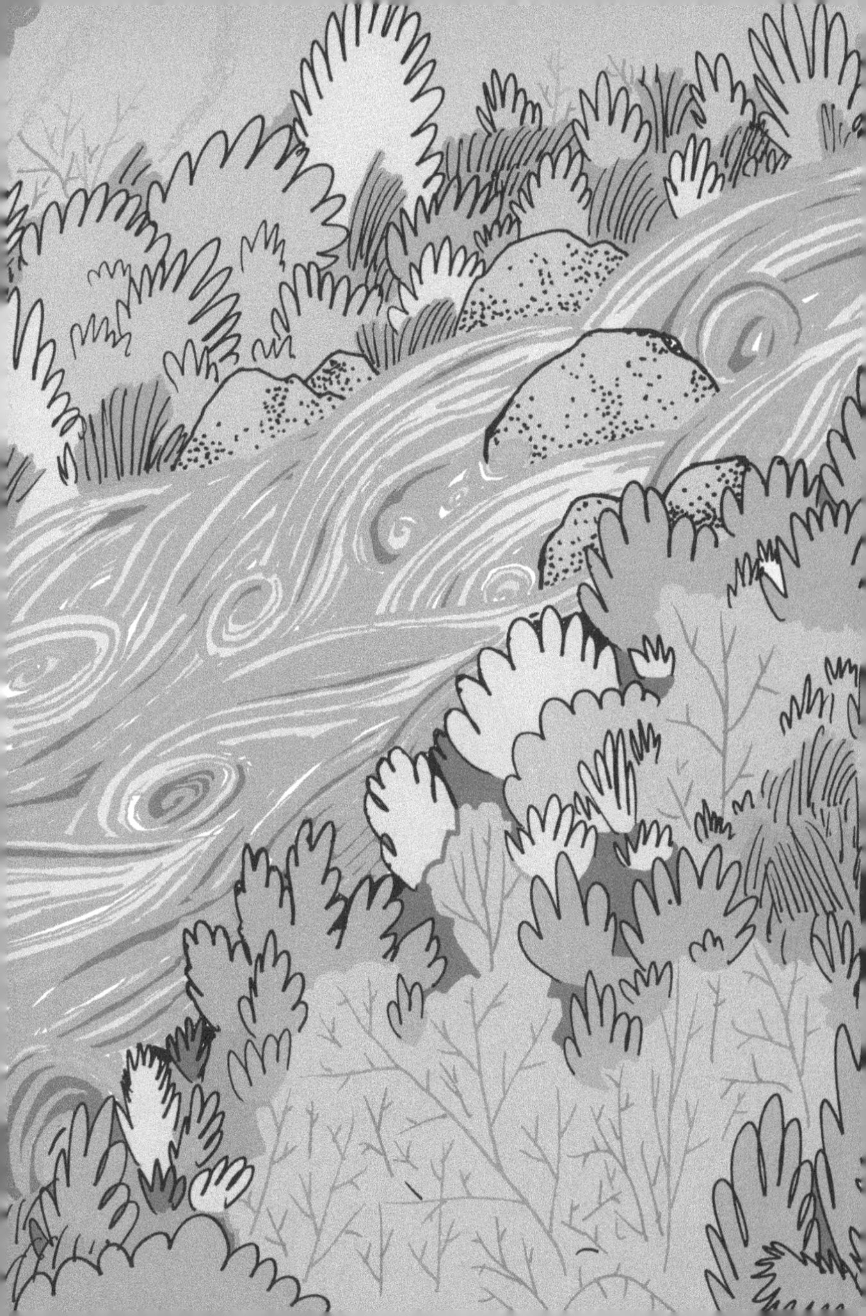

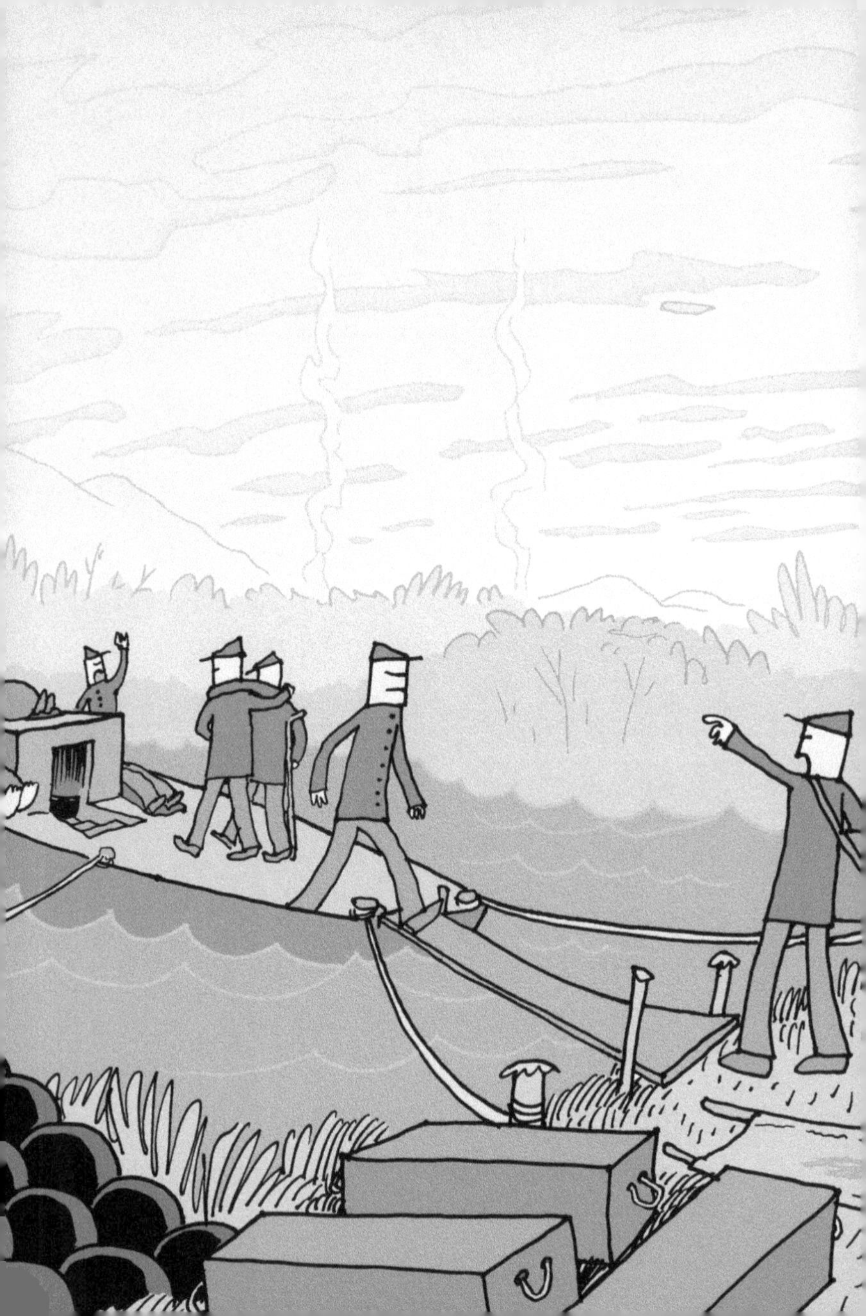

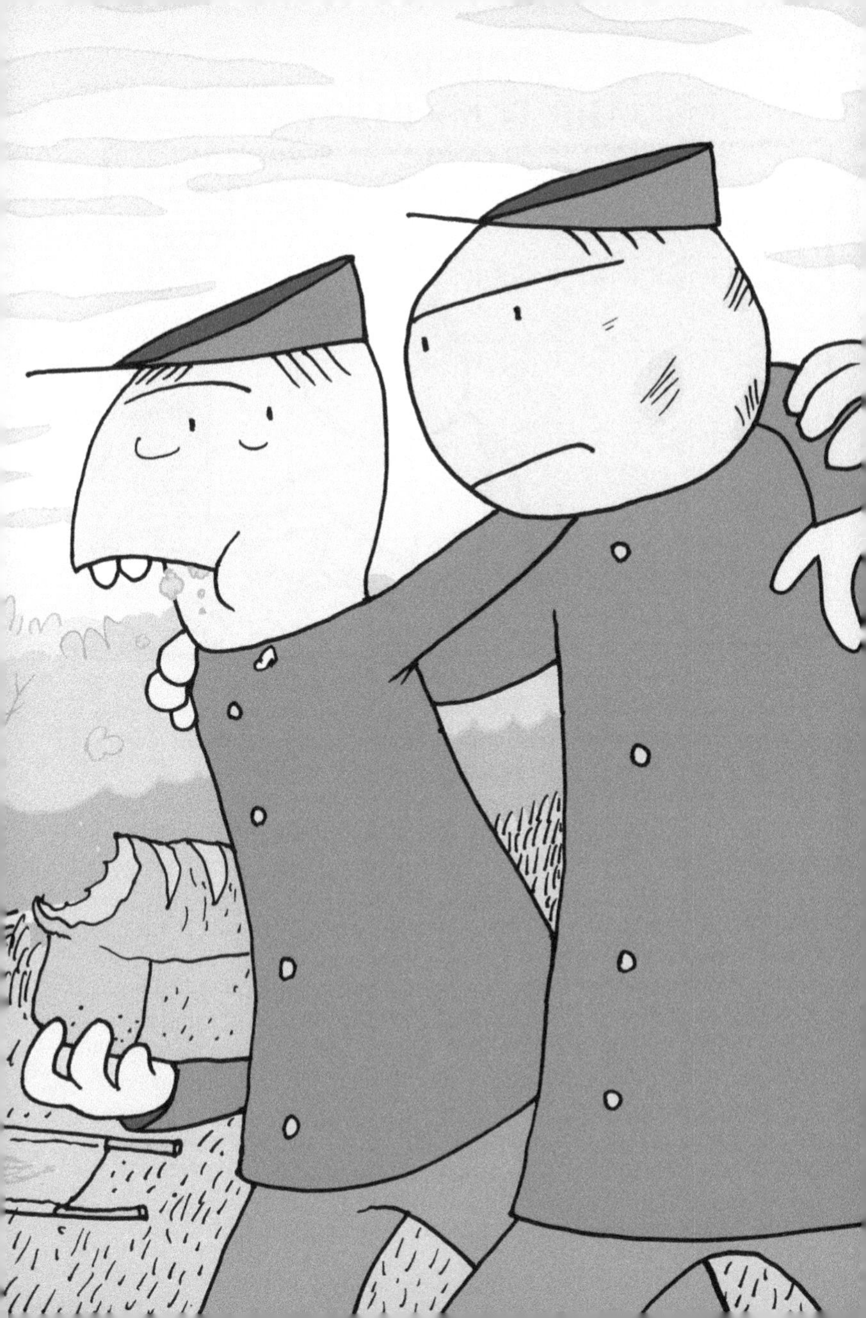

# APPENDIX.
## ABOUT *the* DIARY.

As archived in the Henniker Historical Society Museum at Henniker, NH, The "Diary of Freeman E. Colby" consists of a 31-page single-spaced typewritten transcript fragment detailing Colby's early Civil War experiences (April 1861 to April 1863).

Despite the title, Colby seems not to have composed his "diary" during the years described. The first page (see image) includes a retrospective ode to his beloved wife Margaret Clement, who "has gone on before me but her memory is ever with me." According to her local gravestone, Margaret died in 1906; this dates Colby's text to at least 40 years after the events described.

Throughout this graphic novel adaptation, a tilde (~) under any panel indicates minor revision or adaptation of Colby's text. Ellipses (...) for the most part indicate omission of text deemed unnecessary or irrrelevant in the visual narrative. This edition omits Colby's occasional references to time periods outside 1860-1862. Inserted visual texts derive from period sources; for example, the "WAR NEWS" on page 8 references several *Harper's Weekly* headlines from June-July 1862.

### DIARY OF FREEMAN E. COLBY

When the war broke out I was at home helping my father with the work of the farm. I was then just turned twenty-one. Most of my time after finishing school had been spent there or at school teaching, except a year at New London Academy, which had given me a chance to rub elbows with others of my own age and to get a strong taste of mathematics from that fine old master, Professor Knight, who was so long the presiding genius on New London Hill.

At keeping school I had had good success and in schools where there were many scholars older and larger than myself I had never failed to keep order. Several times I had finished the terms of teachers who had left their school rooms by the window; and as I tried to be just, as well as strict, my services were in demand, particularly in districts where each winter term was expected to commence with a set-to between the Master and a half dozen or more of husky lads whose muscles were toughened by the use of scythe, flail and axe and whose ideas of independence would not permit them to learn of one who could be either frightened or licked. There, the Master and not the scholars had to stand being hazed.

But I was anxious to get some opening that promised better returns than either farming or school keeping and during vacation time I had tried my hand at several other occupations such as stencil-making and silver-plating, but without any great financial success for, though I did good work, being naturally handy with tools, the time taken up in soliciting and delivering orders kept my earnings down.

With the bombardment of Fort Sumpter the whole North awoke with a shock to the existence of war; but few of even the best informed men dreamed of how relentless and long drawn out that struggle was to be. Even the President, in his call for volunteers, only specified 30 days as the length of service.

During that summer and fall there was plenty of work on the farm for us all and I only left occasionally for trips about the nearby towns with large and brightly colored pictures of forts, battle scenes and other patriotic scenes, which found a ready sale. As winter came on my work was less needed at home, but instead of taking a school to keep I went to Woburn and got a job in a currier shop. A former classmate and neighbor, named Jonas Bacon, worked there too but besides him and some of his relatives with whom I went to board, I knew no one in the town.

I was never over ready to make new friends but during the winter I met Margaret Clement, the one woman, who as the years passed, became only dearer to me as friend, sweetheart and wife. No more loyal and helpful, and yet sympathetic and lovable woman ever lived than she. She has gone on before me but her memory is ever with me now as it was in all the long war years and it stands now as it did then for all that is truest and best in the world. She was then learning the tailors trade in the shop of        who made clothes for succeeding generations of Woburn people for more than sixty years.

With Lincoln's first call for troops in 1861, Newton, my brother, was at once wild to join the army. He was only 17 then and everyone told him he was too young to enlist but as time passed he only became more eager to go. Early in the summer of 1862 father and mother saw that in spite of all they could say he was bound to enlist and would run away and join some one of the many regiments being raised from time to time without their consent if they continued to withhold it.

*The first page of the HHS transcript.*
*(Compare with pages 2-9 of this book.)*

# APPENDIX.
# FREEMAN COLBY'S WAR RECORD.

The HHS transcript of Colby's diary includes a cover page listing the following dates for Freeman Colby's Civil War military service:

| <div align="center">**Freeman Eri Colby**</div> | |
|---|---|
| Enlisted    Woburn, Mass. | July 22, 1862 |
| Trained    Lynnfield and Boxford, Mass. to | Aug. 31, 1862 |
| Home without leave – rejoined regiment | Sep. 7, 1862 |
| Arrived Washington | Sep. 9, 1862 |
| Arlington Heights, Va. | Sep. 10-14 |
| Picket duty up the Potomac River<br>        Poolesville – Edwards Ferry to | Apr. 15, 1863 |
| *Guard duty, Washington D.C. to* | *Jul. 20, 1863\** |
| *Active duty – Army of the Potomac*<br>        *Warrenton Junction – Bealton Station*<br>        *Rappahannock Station – Culpepper --*<br>        *2nd Div. Field Hospital on the Rapidan to* | *Oct. 2, 1863* |
| *Patient, Carver Hospital, Washington, except when home on*<br>*furlough Spring of 1864 to* | *Apr. 28, 1864* |
| *Active duty – Virginia Campaign*<br>        *Wilderness – Spottsylvania – Weldon Railroad --*<br>        *Front of Petersburg to* | *Mar. 29, 1865* |
| *March to Washington, D.C. – Journey to Massachusetts*<br>        *Dinwiddie Court House* | *Apr. 2, 1865* |
| *Burksville Junction* | *Apr. 19, 1865* |
| *Arlington Heights, Va.* | *May 12 to 29, 1865* |
| *Readville, Mass.* | *Jun. 6, 1865* |

\* *Italics indicate dates not covered by the HHS diary transcript. Accounts of Colby's later adventures (1863-5) appear in his Civil War letters, also archived by HHS alongside the diary fragment.*

# APPENDIX.
# REFERENCE IMAGES & SOURCES.

Drawing Colby's narrative as a comic involved equal parts imagination, careful reading of similar accounts, and reference to numerous period visual sources. This section collects some favorite source images.

p.6: *"With the bombardment of Fort Sumter..."* ~ Detail from a Currier & Ives lithograph, "Bombardment of Fort Sumter, Charleston Harbor: 12th & 13th of April, 1861" (detail) (1861?) [LOC.gov]

p.7: *"I knew no one in the town."* ~ Lyceum Hall, Woburn, MA (undated photo) [www.yeoldewoburn.net]

COLONEL P. STEARNS DAVIS

p.10 ~ Col. P. Stearns Davis
[archive.org]

p.14 ~ Captain John I. Richardson
[www.yeoldewoburn.net]

p.27: *"took a horsecar to Winchester"* ~ Horse-drawn streetcars appear in this Harpers' Weekly's illustration, "Rebel Prisoners leaving Baltimore for Fortress Monroe" (detail) (1861) [loc.gov]

p.39: *"We took dinner"* ~ Detail from the lithograph, "Union Volunteer Refreshment Saloon of Philadelphia" (T. Sinclair's Lith., 1861) [loc.gov]

p.47: *"Early next morning we marched six miles through Pennsylvania Avenue"* ~ Alfred Waud's sketch, "Great War Meeting at Washington, District of Columbia, August 6, 1862," showing the unfinished Capitol dome past which Colby & co. may have marched. [loc.gov]

p.48: *"The whole city of Washington lay spread out before us"* ~ Lithograph by Fitz Henry Lane, c.1838: "View of the city of Washington, the metropolis of the United States of America, taken from Arlington House..." (detail) [loc.gov]

p.49: *"Shot in an Alexandria hotel"* ~ "Death of Ellsworth" (detail, steel engraving, c.1862) [loc.gov] – According to the item summary: *"James T. Jackson, proprietor of the Marshall House Tavern in Alexandria, Va. shooting and killing Col. Elmer E. Ellsworth, of the 11th N.Y. Fire Zouaves. Jackson was immediately killed by Pvt. Frances E. Brownell, 1861 May 24."*

p.50: *"Nearby was the homestead of Robert E. Lee"* ~ "Arlington House, east front, June 28, 1864" by Andrew J. Russell [loc.gov]

p.52: *"The day before we arrived..."* ~ "The battle of Groveton or Second Bull Run" (drawing by Edwin Forbes, 1862) [loc.gov]

p.53: *"A dozen men killed at chain bridge"* ~ Wartime photograph:
"Washington, District of Columbia. Chain bridge" [loc.gov]

p.151: *"Even there the care was none too good"* ~ Alfred Waud's sketch,
"Hospital tent, Harrisons landing, Surgeon Boyd" (1862?) [loc.gov]

p.82: *"We had no shelter except our blankets, so we had to make the most of these."* ~ "Private Charles H. Osgood of Company C, 16th New Hampshire Infantry Regiment with stenciled blanket and forage cap" (1861) [loc.gov]

p.160: *"My stomach craved more food"* ~ Edwin Forbes' "Fall in for soup –
company mess" (c.1876), from "Life Studies of the Great Army" [loc.gov]

p.161: *"Only the strongest teeth"* ~ "Preparing the Mess," from a wartime
stereograph by Mathew Brady, in "Camp Scenes. Army of the Potomac." [loc.gov]

p.163: *"A single smell was a great plenty."* ~ Detail from wartime photograph, "Petersburg, Va. Sutler's tent, 2d Division, 9th Corps" (c.1864) [loc.gov]

p.164: *"These were strictly cash prices"* ~ Arthur Lumley's olive paper drawing: "A sutler's tent near H.Q." (August 1862) [loc.gov]

p.166: *"To pay for laundry"* ~ "Washington, District of Columbia. Tent life of the 31st Penn. Inf. (later, 82d Penn. Inf.) at Queen's farm..." (detail) [loc.gov]

p.168: *"The tent was damp"* ~ "Group of soldiers of Company G, 71st New York Vols. In front of 'Sibley' tent" (detail) (1861) [loc.gov]

p.173: *"Camp Desolation"* ~ "Rainy Day in Camp" (detail)
(Winslow Homer, 1871) [wikimedia.org]

p.190: *"Spent an hour trying to get him to
sing a song"* ~ General Cuvier Grover
(detail) [loc.gov]

p. 225: *"Just then Lieutenant Tidd
came along..."* ~ Detail of 1ˢᵗ Lt.
Luke R. Tidd [39th Reg. MA
Volunteer Infantry, Company "K"
Records, www.yeoldewoburn.net]

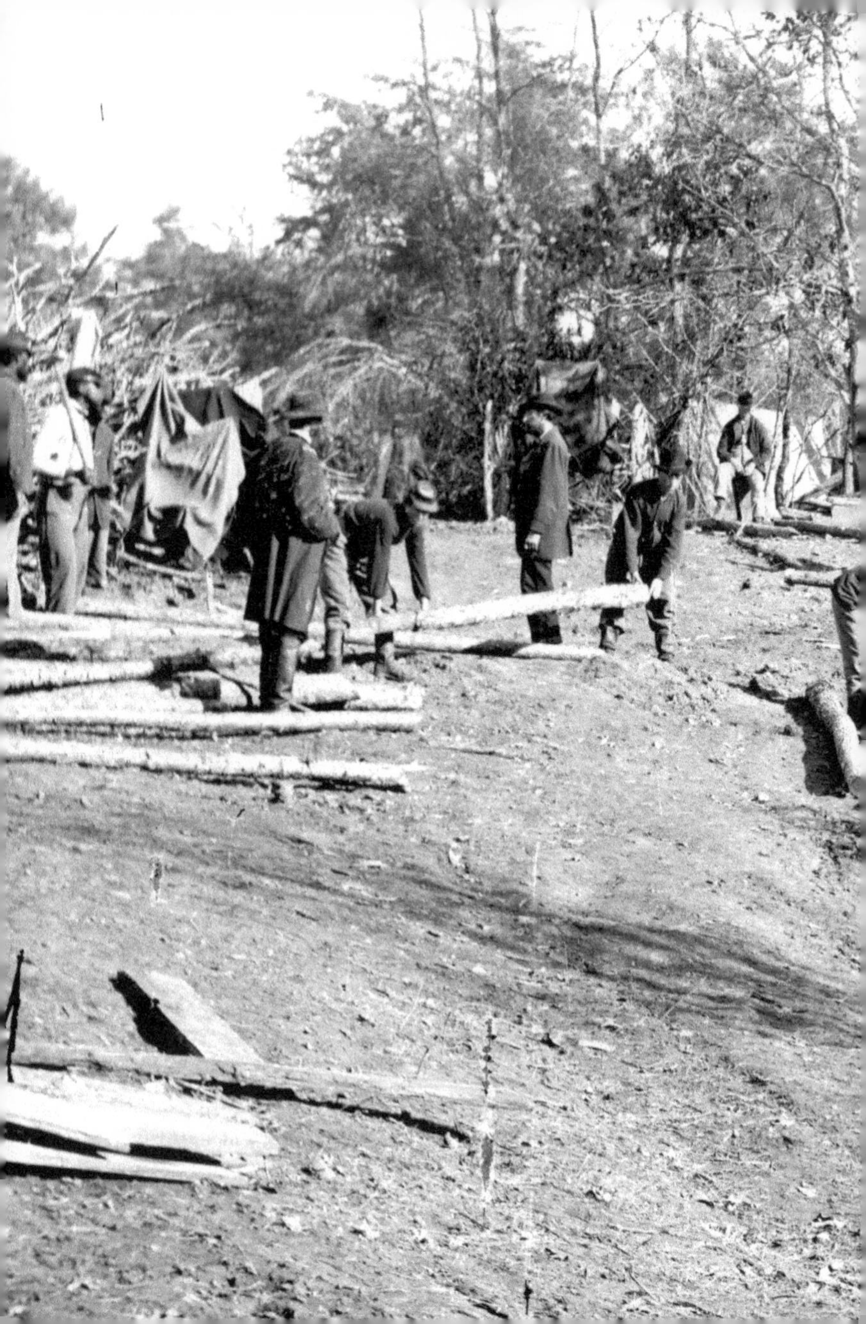

p.200: *"We had got our tents fairly well fixed up for winter"* ~
From a wartime glass stereograph: "James River, Virginia.
Building winter quarters, Ft. Brady" [loc.gov]
SEE ALSO: p. 104: *"I have often watched the blacks..."*

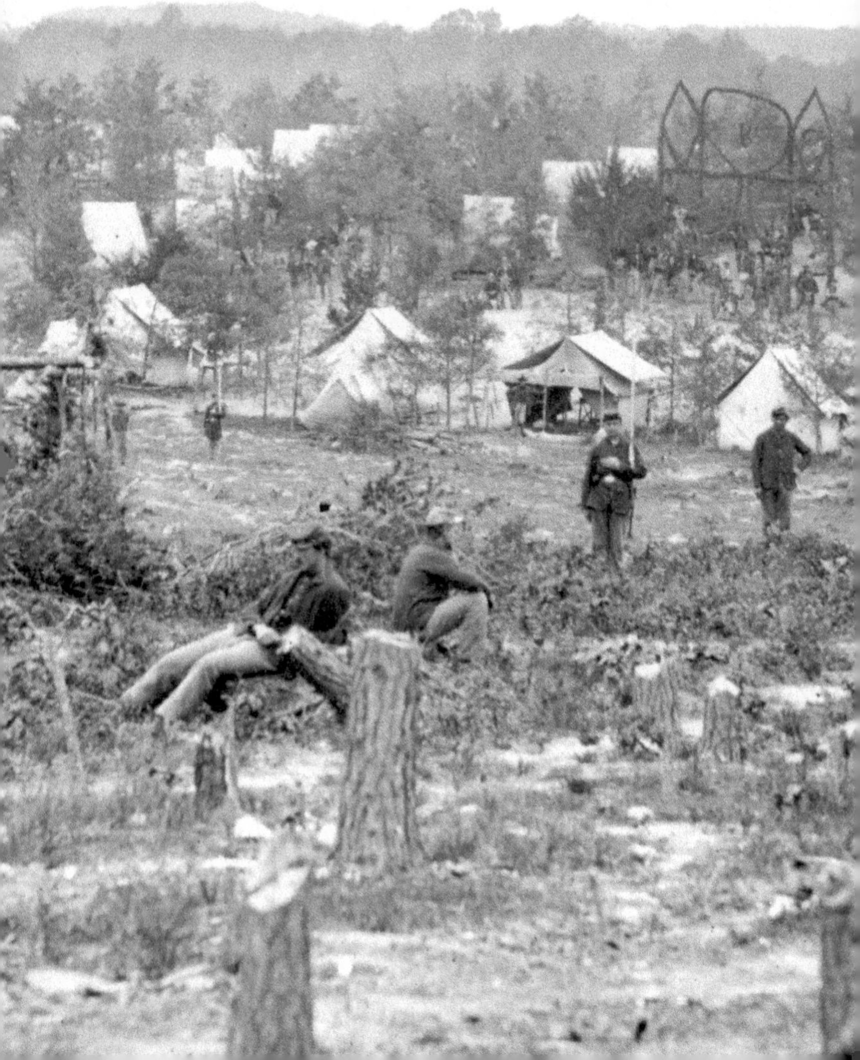

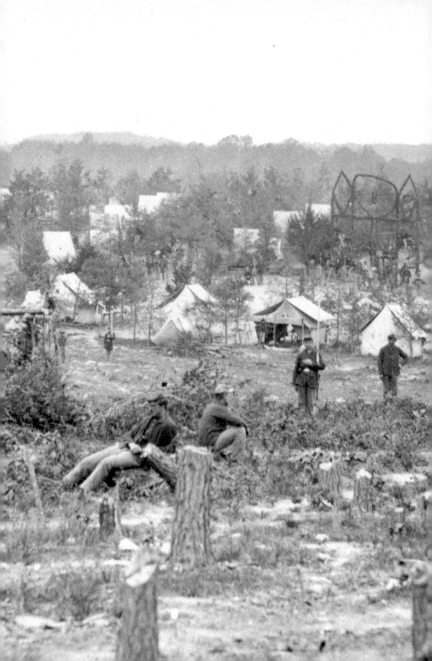

p.248: *"While the good weather held, we made use of it."* ~
"Camp of 30th Pennsylvania Infantry" (detail) [loc.gov] ~
This jaunty wartime regimental portrait displays the creative
care put into camp improvement and decoration; it also hints
at the sheer amount of woodcutting involved in army life.

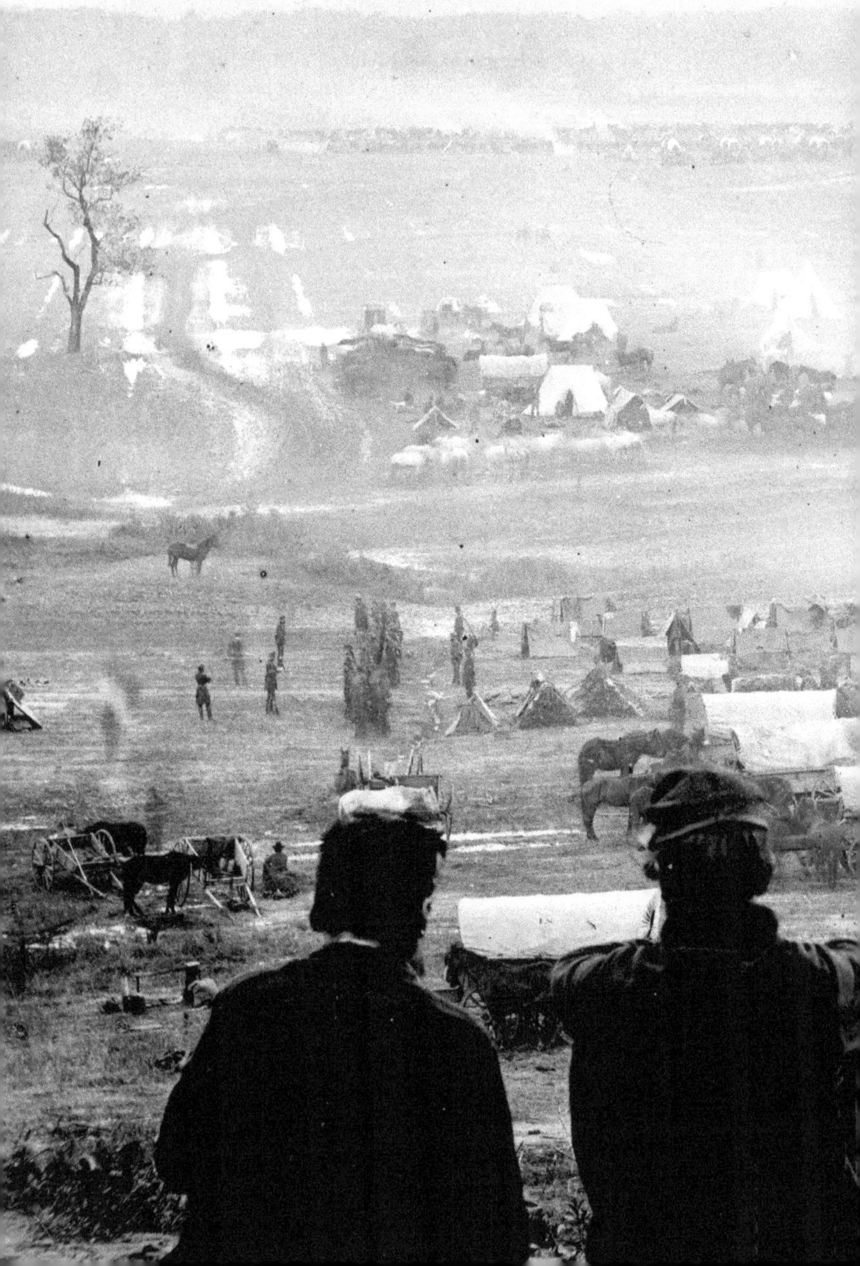

p.272: *"Muddy fields outside the camp, and muddy streets within it."* ~ Photograph by James Gibson, May 1862: "Cumberland Landing, Va. Federal encampment on Pamunkey River, Va.; another view" (detail) [loc.gov]

The Reveille

Going to Camp

p.273: *"Trains of heavy army wagons toiled along axle deep in mud..."* ~ 1862 sketches by Alfred Waud: "Why the Army of the Potomac doesn't move" [loc.gov]. Section titles: "The Relief / Going to Camp / Difficulties of Teaming / King Mud in camp"

Difficulties of Teaming

p.240: *"Their holidays only commenced the 25th..."* ~ Illustration from Frank Leslie's Illustrated Newspaper: "Winter holidays in the southern states. Plantation frolic on Christmas Eve" (1857) [loc.gov]. Note white spectators, band, &c.

p.254: *"There came a perfect deluge of boxes"* ~ Illustration by Charles W. Reed: "A Wagon-Load of Boxes" from p. 220 of John D. Billings' *Hardtack and Coffee, or, The Unwritten Story of Army Life* (1887) [archive.org]. Billings' account, & Reed's illustrations therein, have aided immensely in this project.

p.277: *"Burnside was making another attempt..."* ~ Photograph by Alexander Gardner: "Warrenton, Va. Gen. Ambrose E. Burnside & staff; another view" (detail) (Nov. 1862) [loc.gov].

RÉVEILLÉ.

p.286: *"I got a fife and blew the reveille"* ~ The familiar bugle call summoning infantry units to morning inspection, as given on p.168 of Billings' *Hardtack and Coffee* (1887) [archive.org].

Marek Bennett draws comics and plays music wherever he goes. He grew up in Henniker, NH, just across town from Freeman Colby's old home. His webcomic *"Live Free And Draw"* explores forgotten stories from New Hampshire history. He plays Civil War era banjo music with his band, The Hardtacks.

www.MarekBennett.com

~

**Also by Marek Bennett:**
*Hour 72!*
*Breakfast at Mimi's*
*Nicaragua Comics Travel Journal*
*Slovakia: Fall in the Heart of Europe*